AF395625

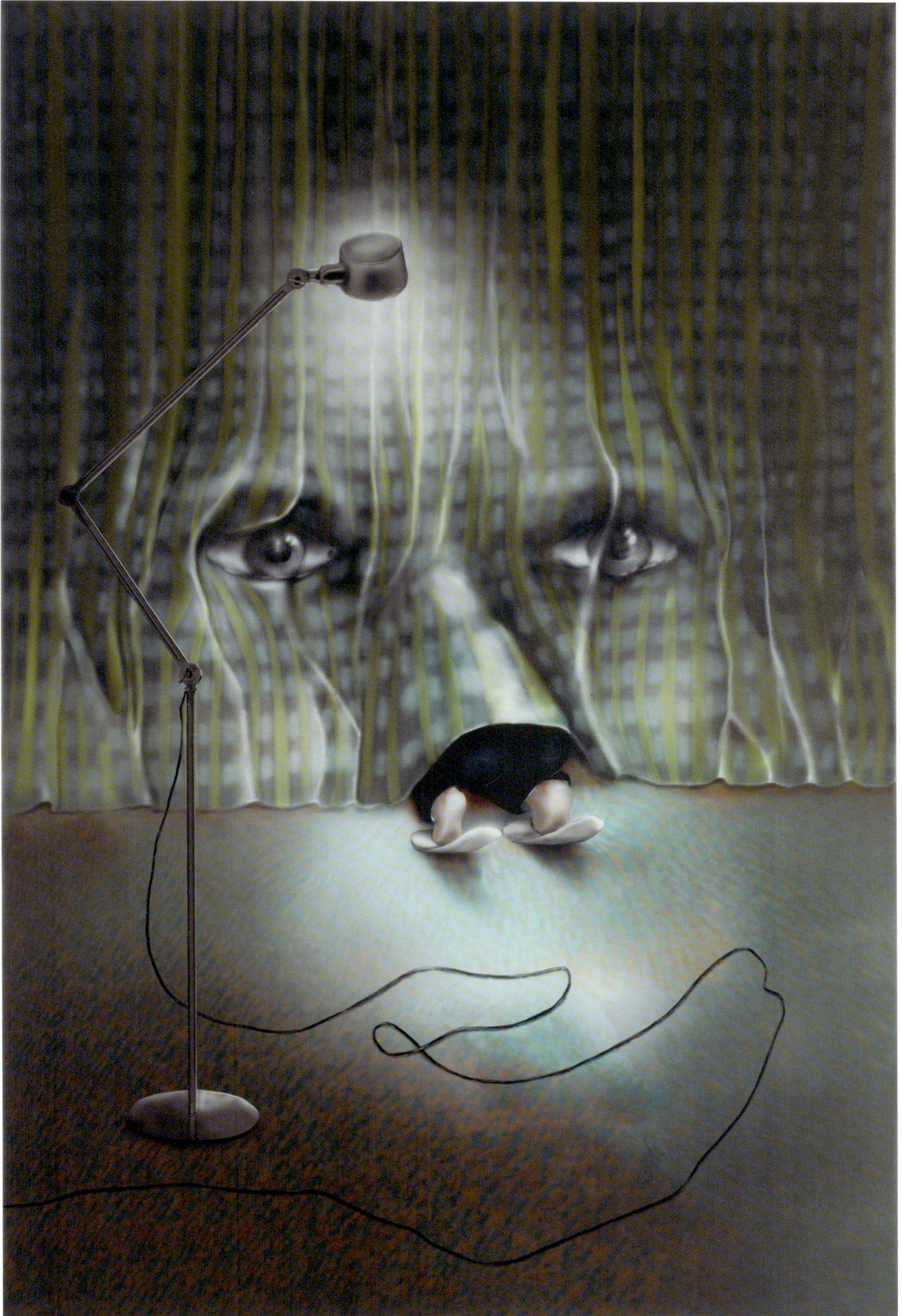

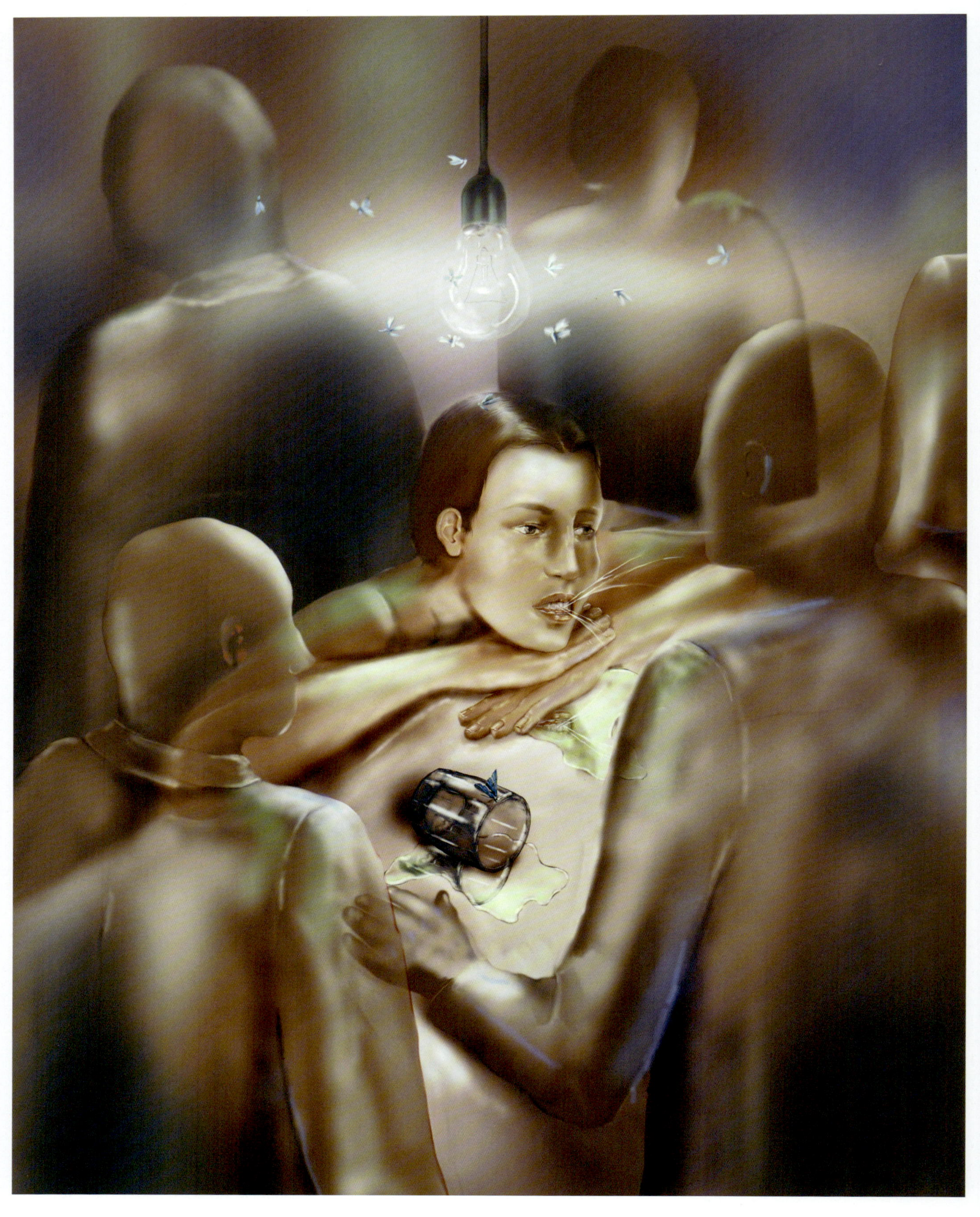

    ← *Curtain Call*, 2020   *Lightheaded*, 2020

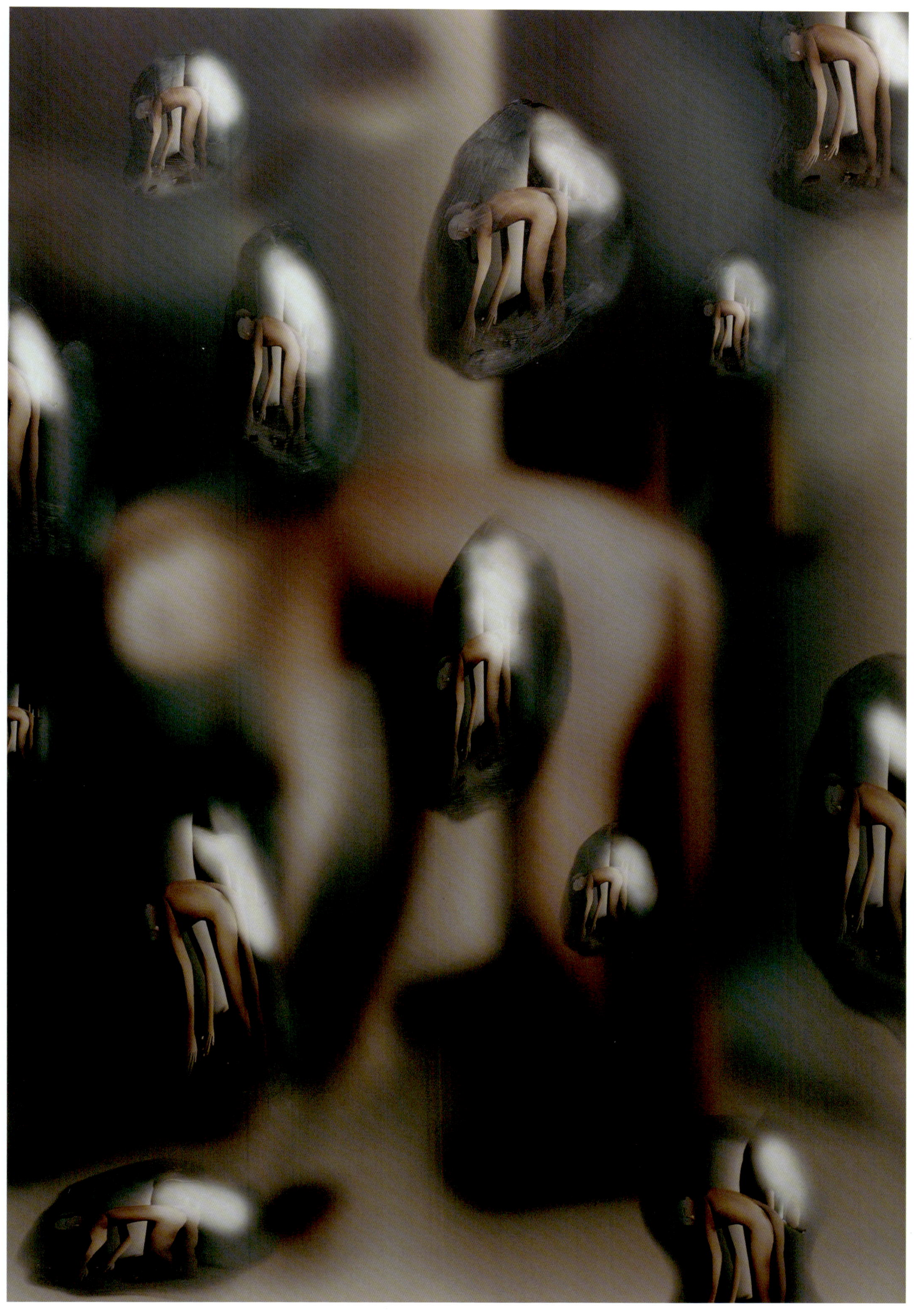

    9:30pm (Dropped and Dripping), 2016

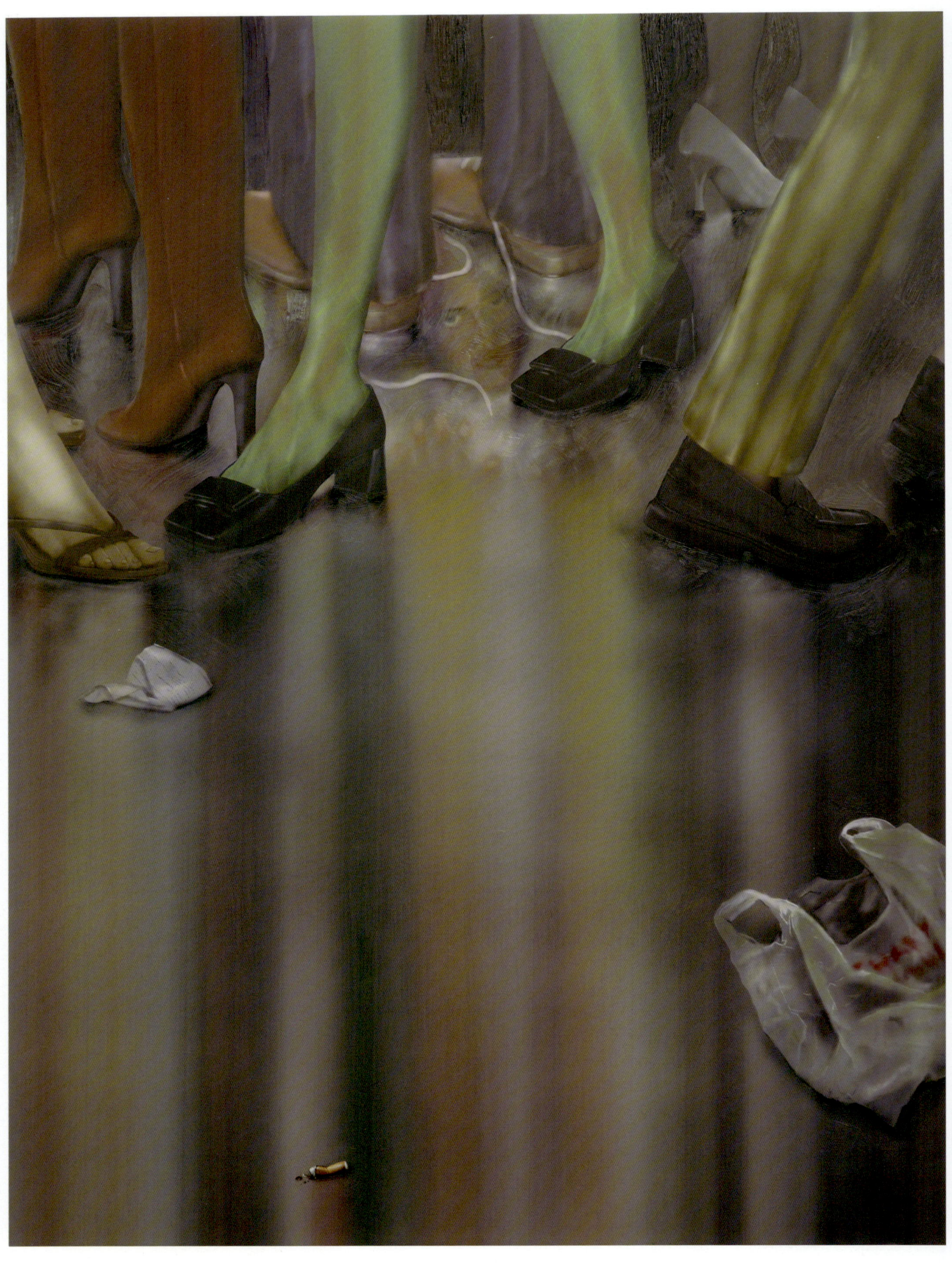

4   *Out of Bounds*, 2021

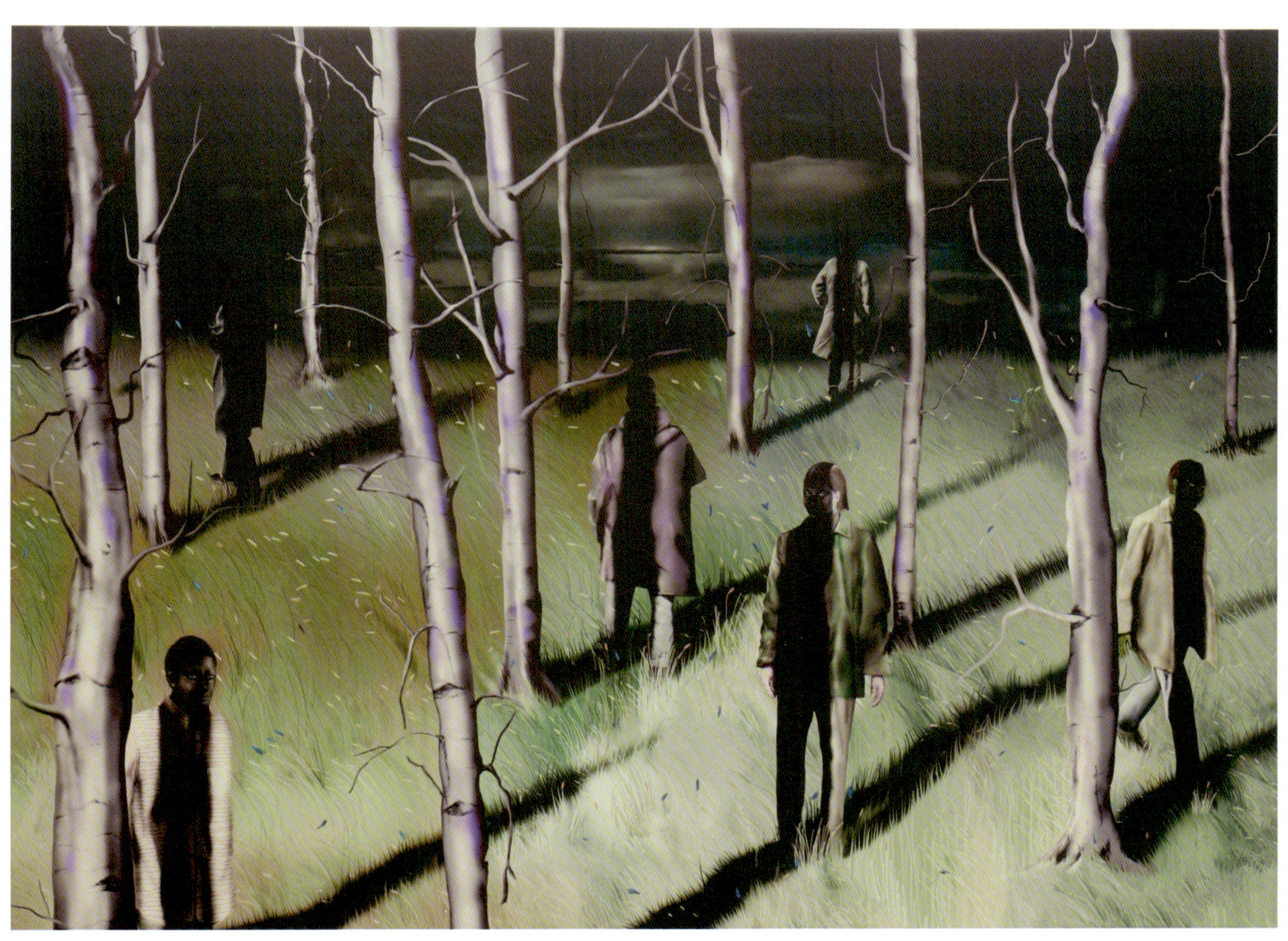

     Murmurs in the Shade, 2021

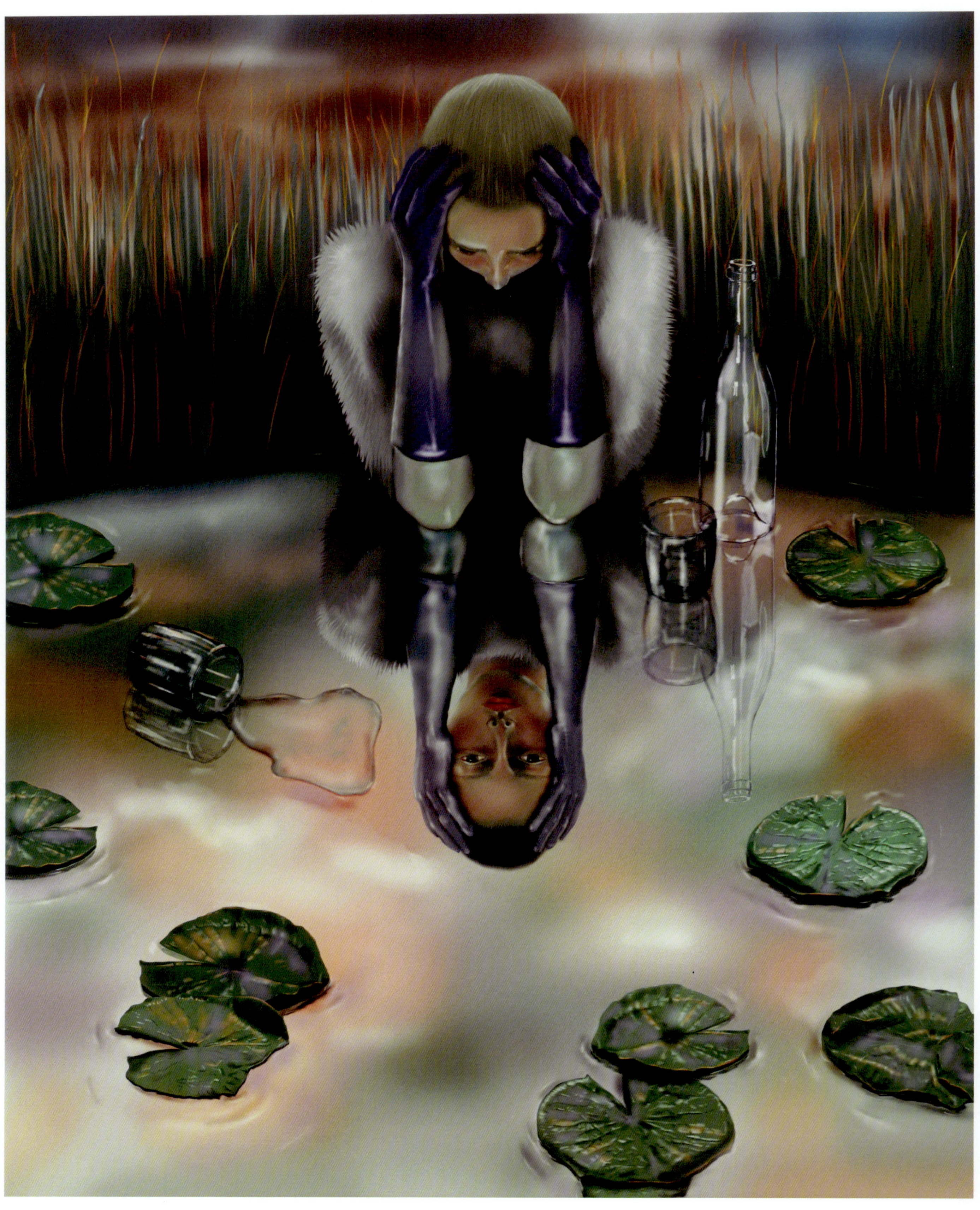

    Reflecting, 2021

LOUISA GAGLIARDI

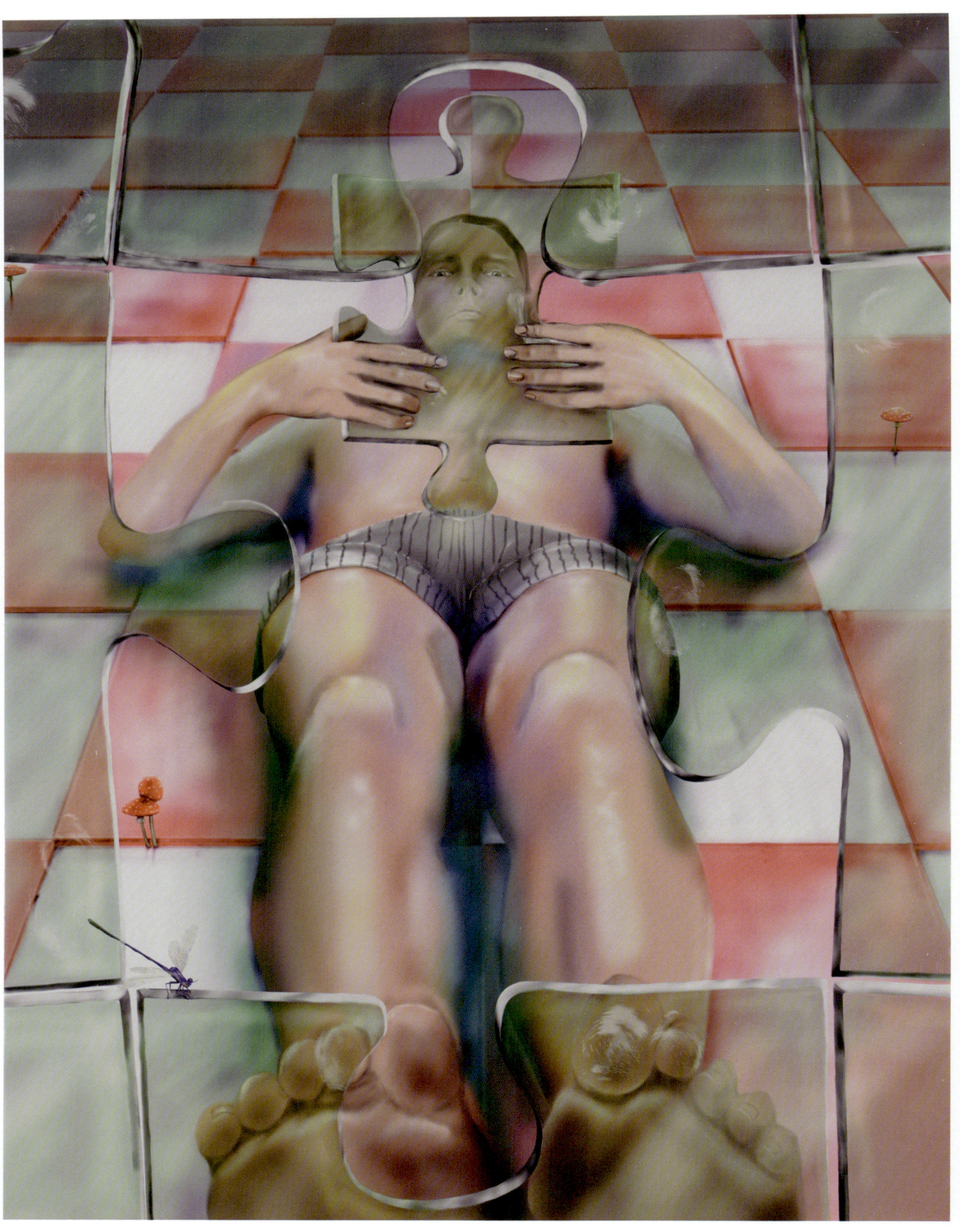

   Late in the Game, 2021

OCULUS RIFT

I could not lay my hands on the notes from my conversation with Louisa Gagliardi until I typed "Mantegna" into my computer's search box. It was this name that came back to me after considerable effort, probably because when we spoke in January, the Early Renaissance artist's name would not come to mind. The painting *Late in the Game* (2021) is freely inspired by the foreshortened body in Mantegna's *Lamentation over the Dead Christ* (c. 1480). Gagliardi's character has grimy nails like Caravaggio's *Mary Magdalen in Ecstasy* (1606), another source with a strong pull for Gagliardi. Louisa told me she approaches bodies like landscapes, taking them at times into the realm of the grotesque.

Fascination is the word that leaps to mind when looking at her work. The type of fascination that verges on revulsion, paradoxically making you want to see more, because your gaze has never seen the like. While the image might be repellent, it remains magnetic, forcing you to confront it. "Like a skin," the images are printed on vinyl, stretched, then reworked with a brush using varnishes and gels that shimmer in the light, as well as glitter and latex, to generate an unsettling sense of depth.

The tangled perspectives create an uncanny impression of flatness, evoking Photoshop's "flatten" function. The protagonist of *Late in the Game* lies on a chequerboard floor of grubby raspberry and mint tiles, echoing the software's "transparent" background. Between the loose tiles grow cartoon mushrooms, behind a screen shaped like a gigantic glass jigsaw puzzle. The man's clumsy hands are holding a puzzle piece close to his creepy avatar face. On the brink of the void perches a purple dragonfly, its wings dangerously close to becoming trapped in the interstice. Fingerprints on my computer overlay the unwashed toes.

Louisa Gagliardi's canvases are frequently generated by digitally layering subjects in parallel at various scales on various pictorial fronts, calling on a range of aesthetic registers with a high-handed urgency untethered from the desire to please. Downgraded photorealism jostles happily with beauty-salon Gothic. Resident Evil clashes with the surrealist Yves Tanguy (1900–1955), while the principle of "composition by multiplying contrast" theorized by Fernand Léger (1881–1955) is augmented by digital means.

The "Pique-niques Sauvages" series (2019, see p. 24–25) cleverly combines the same elements. Thick slices of raw salmon float at times over white backgrounds like supermarket adverts. Blending into the marbled fat are silhouetted figures of men at rest after a celebratory meal, wearing boater hats that seem to situate them in a Renoir painting. The wine glasses are tipped over, their limbs sometimes dislocated, one man seems to be drowning in the ripples that are like a threatening wave.

Auguste Renoir's 1880–1881 *Luncheon of the Boating Party* is a shadowy presence in this series of Gagliardi's painting, as are Pierre et Charles in their 2015 portrait (*Pierre & Charles*, 2015, see p. 59). They are unrecognizable, yet somehow it is clearly them. They are on the surface, smoke wreathing their faces, their arms tangled, fingernails blue as sapphires, though the result is untroubling. It really is them, twisting like the journalist Sylvia von Harden painted by Otto Dix in 1926—brilliant fops.

Louisa Gagliardi has recently turned back to sculpture, mostly flat, as if steamrollered or cut out of a canvas. Her 2021 Swiss Art Awards installation (see p. 56–57) featured three such works—two sad dogs and a green-skinned woman wearing striped pyjamas, hinting at detention camps. Fake chains fastened them to fake candles, yet the impression of unease was very real. A single twitch, and the synthetic carpet would catch alight.

In the 1994 film *Disclosure*, Michael Douglas plays a Seattle businessman who dismantles a sinister corporate plot mounted by Demi Moore and the Malaysian government, using a virtual reality headset very similar in appearance to the Oculus Rift revealed to great fanfare by Facebook almost 20 years later. The name chosen for the supposedly futuristic device is as surprising as the lack of development in the design of a tool that is meant to help people escape their humdrum lives. Maybe the name was intended as a homage to the trompe l'oeil oculus in the Camera degli Sposi at the Ducal Palace in Mantua, painted by Mantegna in the second half of the 15th century, itself an imitation of the real oculus in the Pantheon in Rome. Mantegna's fake blue sky, edged with medallions bearing imperial portraits and foreshortened putti, invites contemplation, almost drawing visitors up and out through it.

Louisa Gagliardi's images are a fascinating cold fusion of disparate worlds and endless shifts between reality and simulacrum. They do not explain: they appeal and absorb. As Louisa Gagliardi says, the pictorial charge of her works is "not illustrative, not narrative, just evocative."

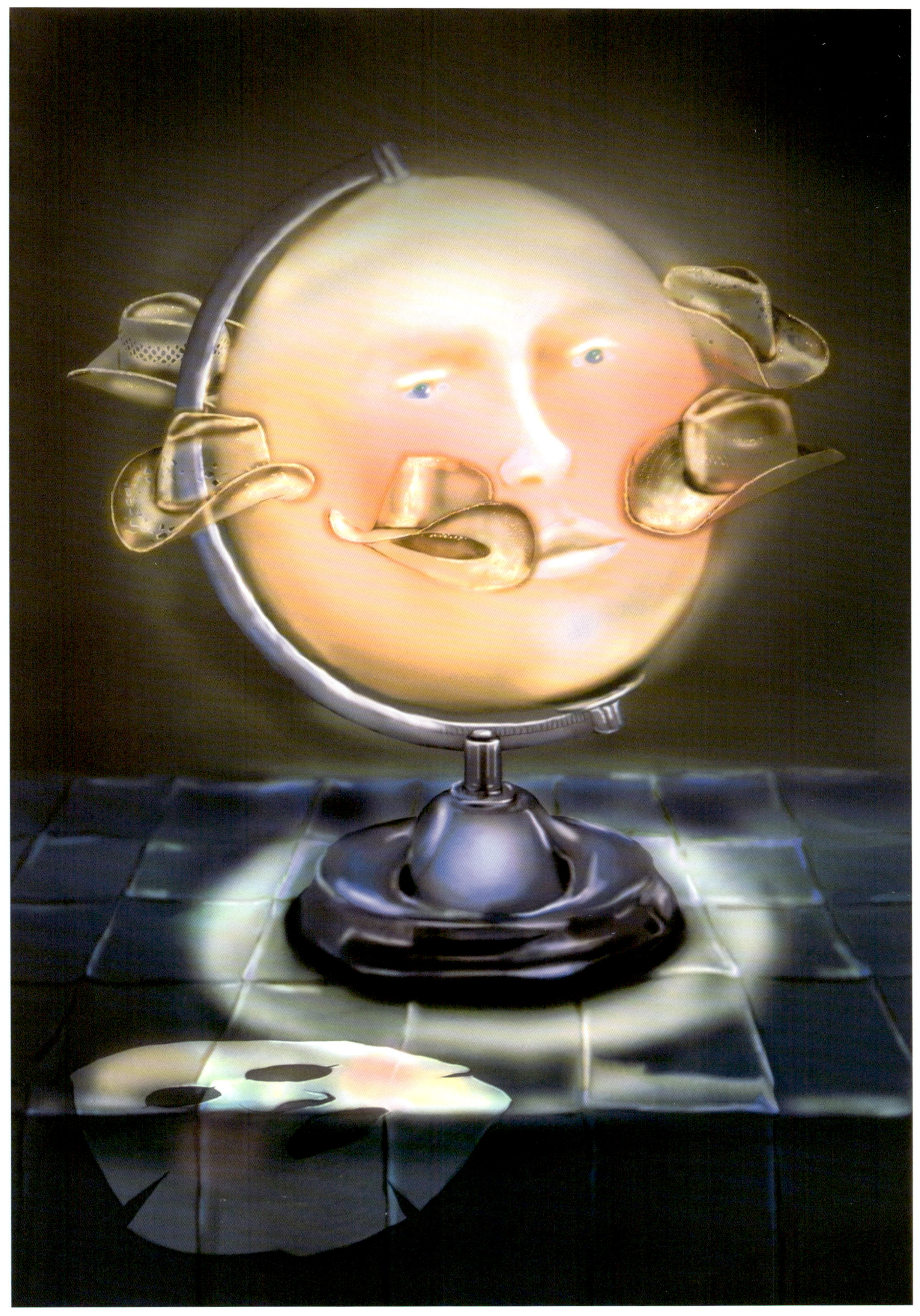

11   *Jet Lag*, 2019

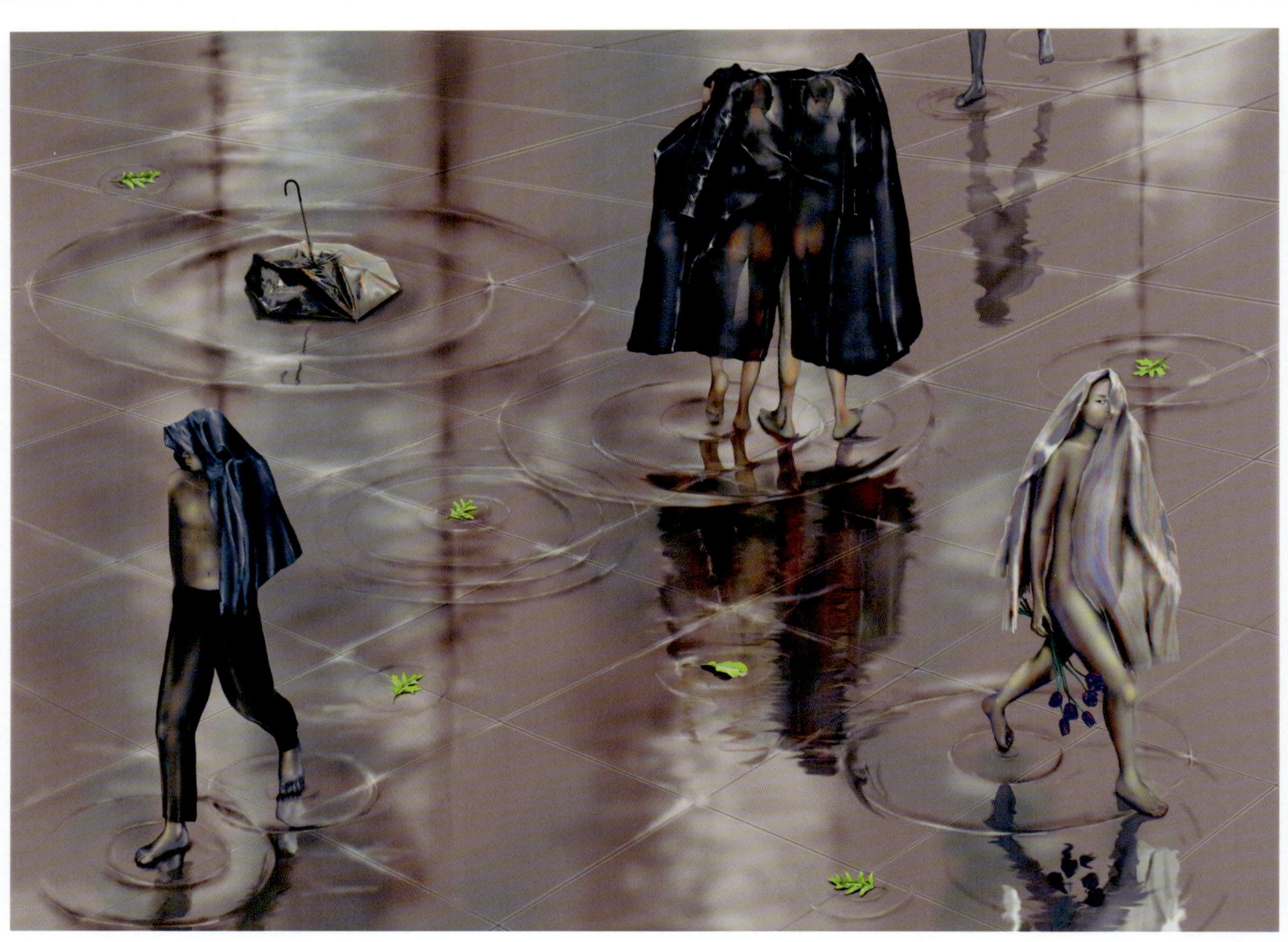

    Undercover, 2022

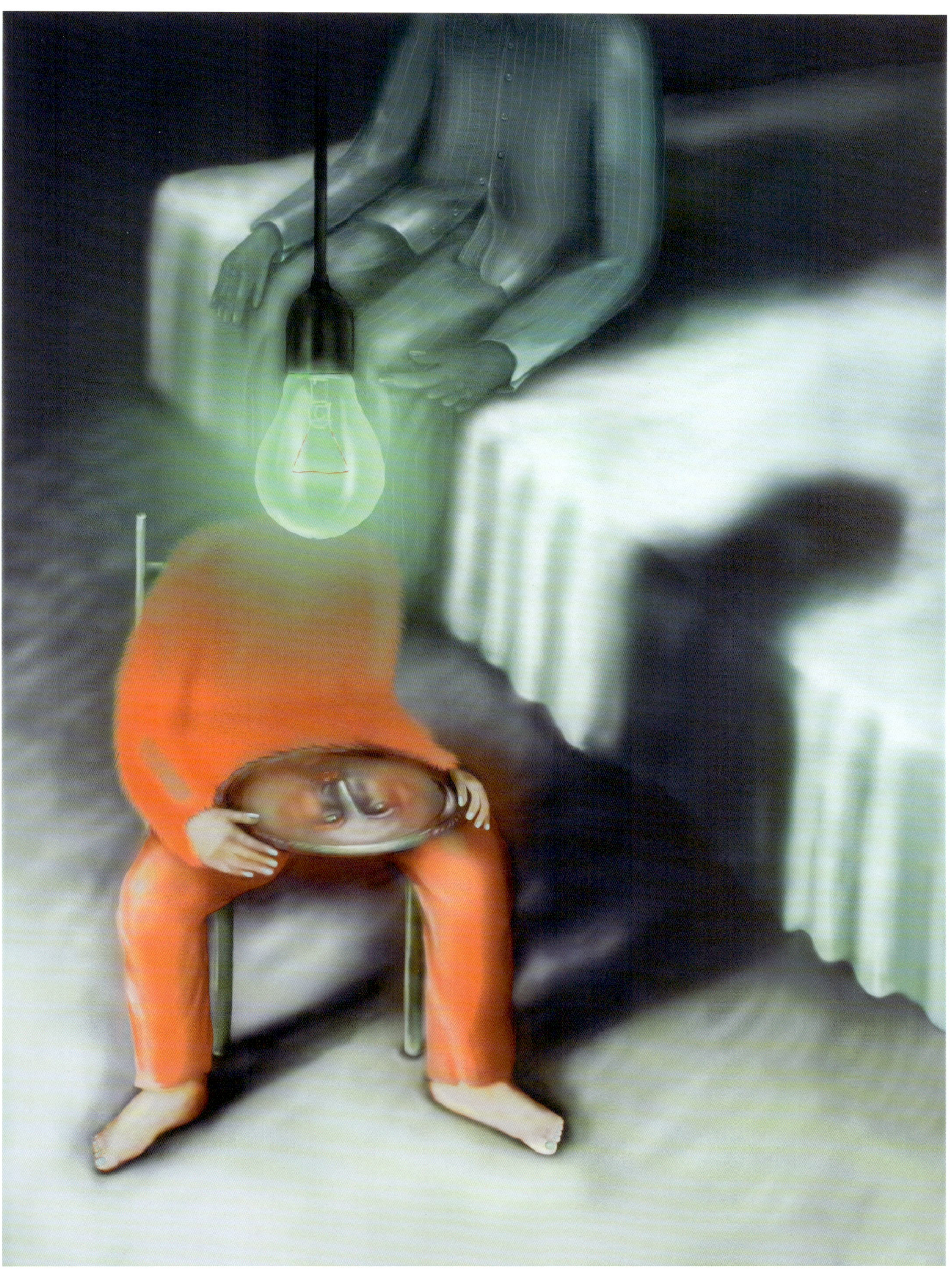

  On a Platter, 2020

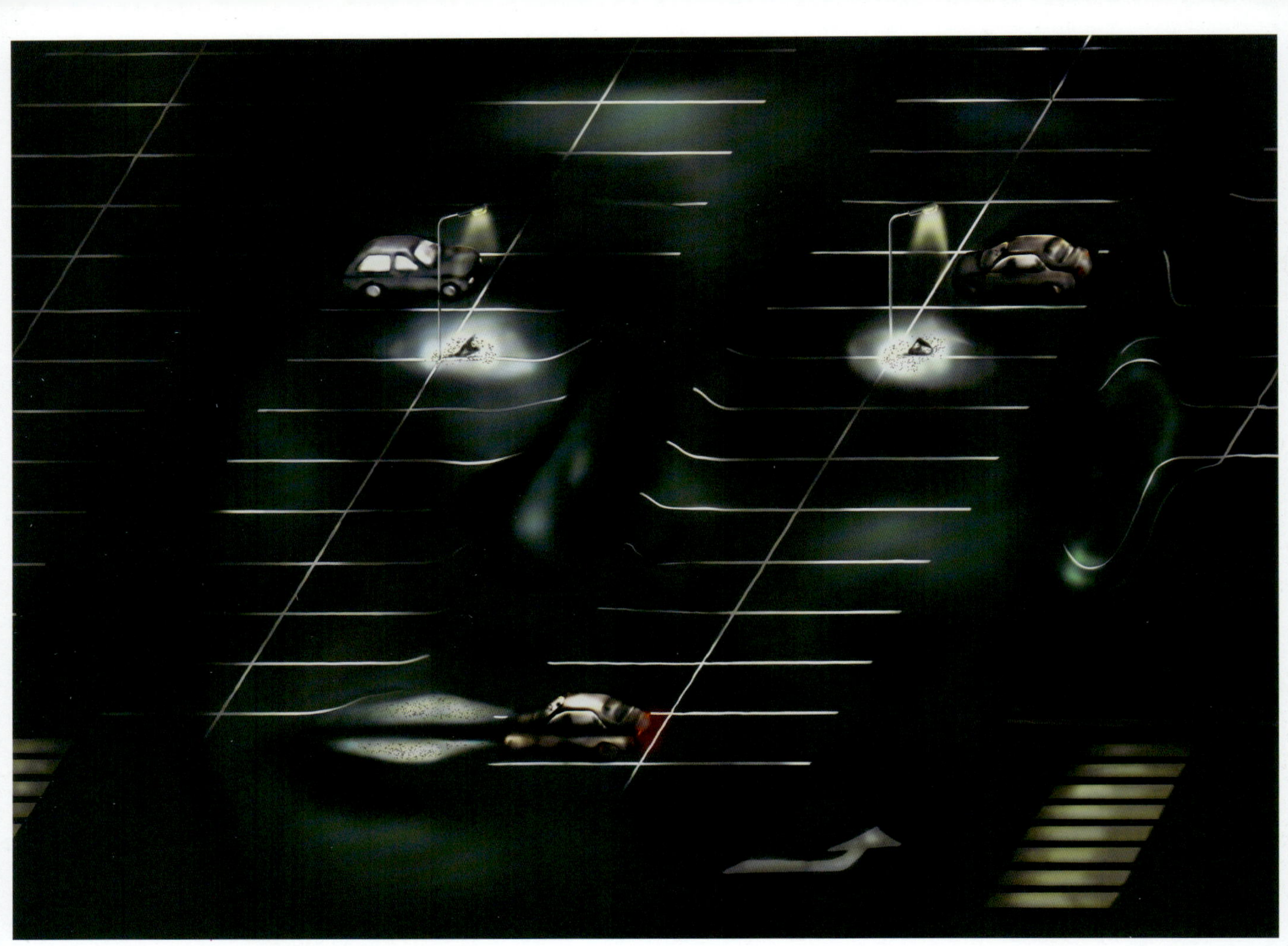

14   *Blind Spot*, 2018

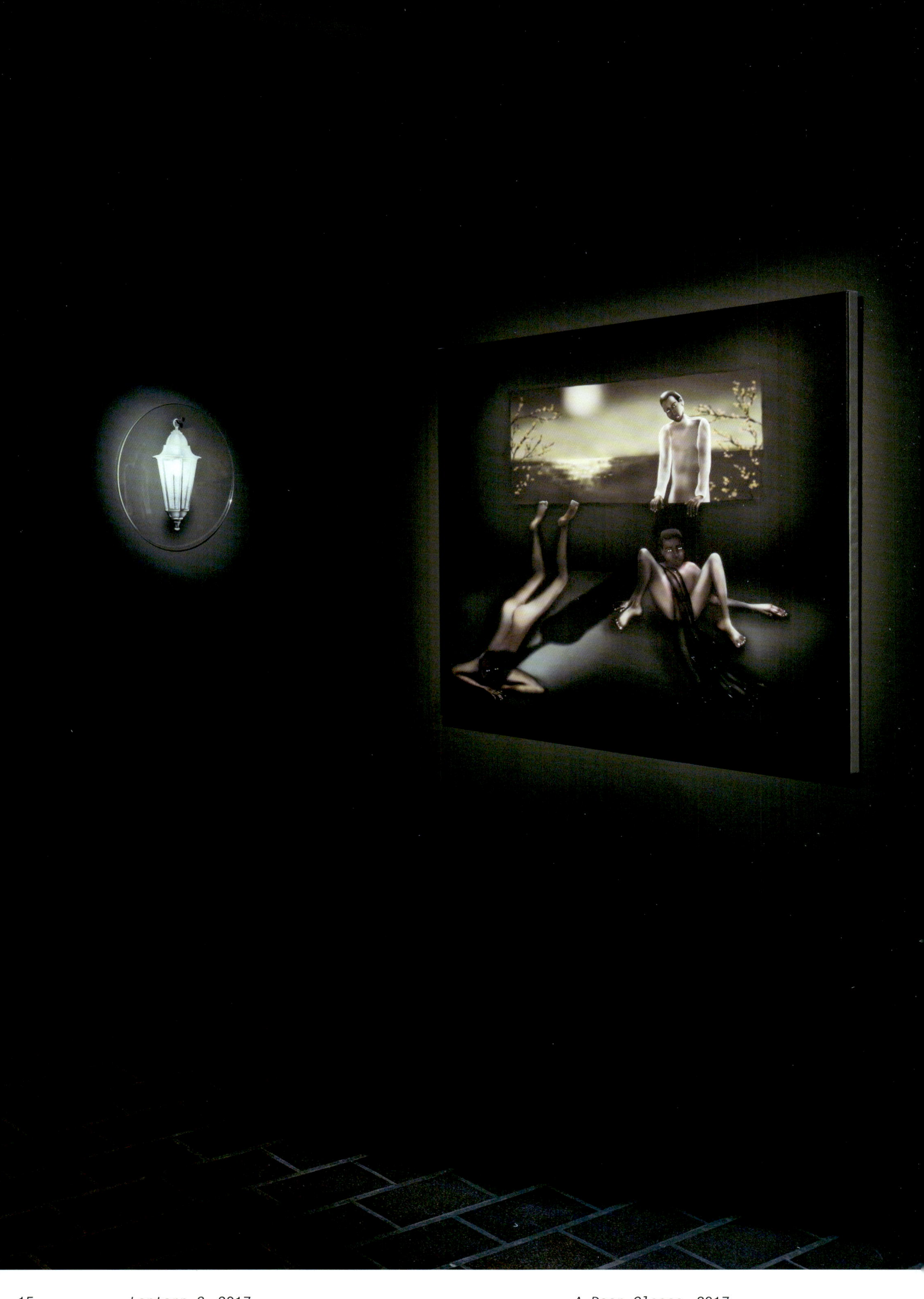

  Lantern 2, 2017   *A Door Closes, 2017*

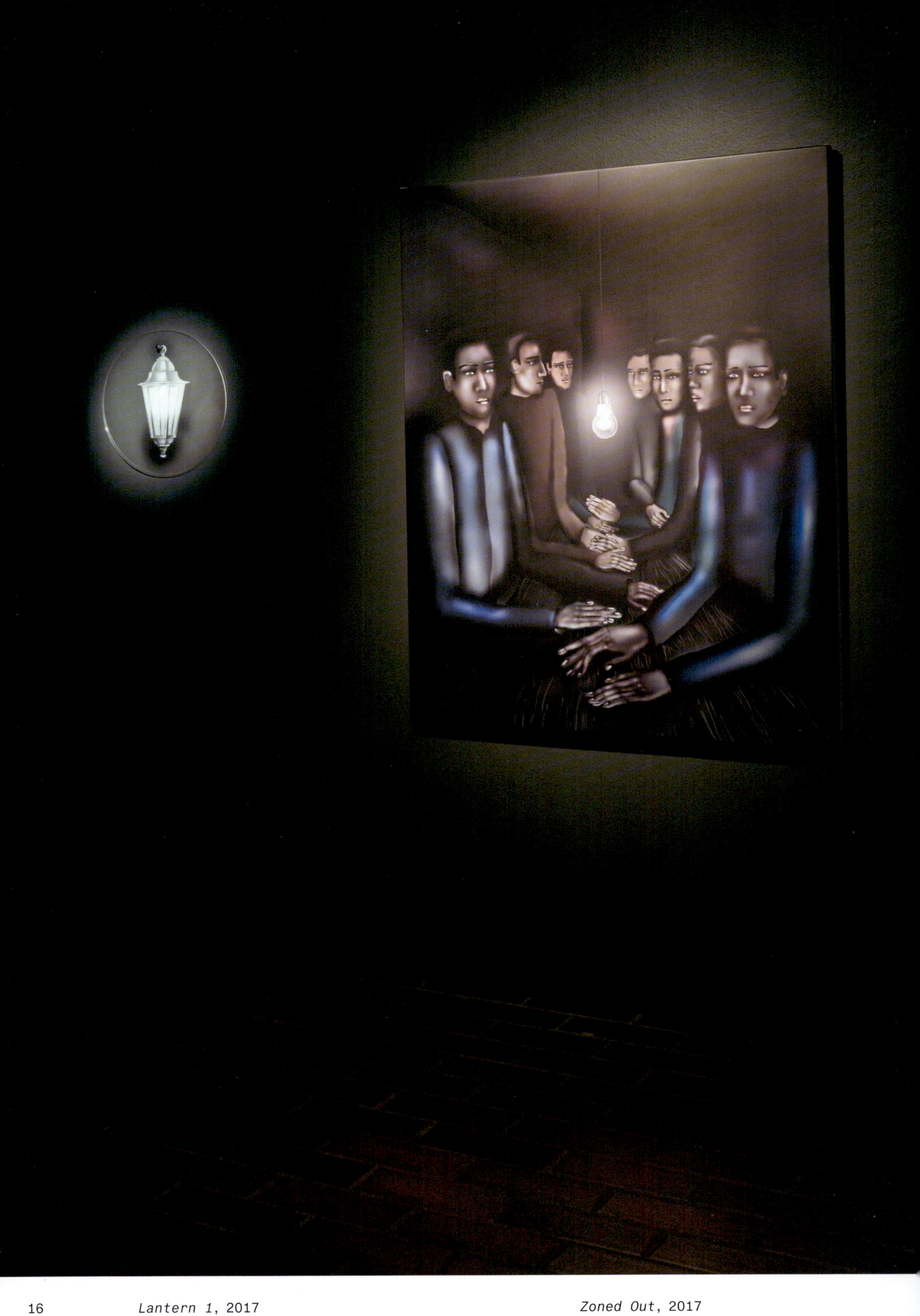

 Lantern 1, 2017   *Zoned Out, 2017*

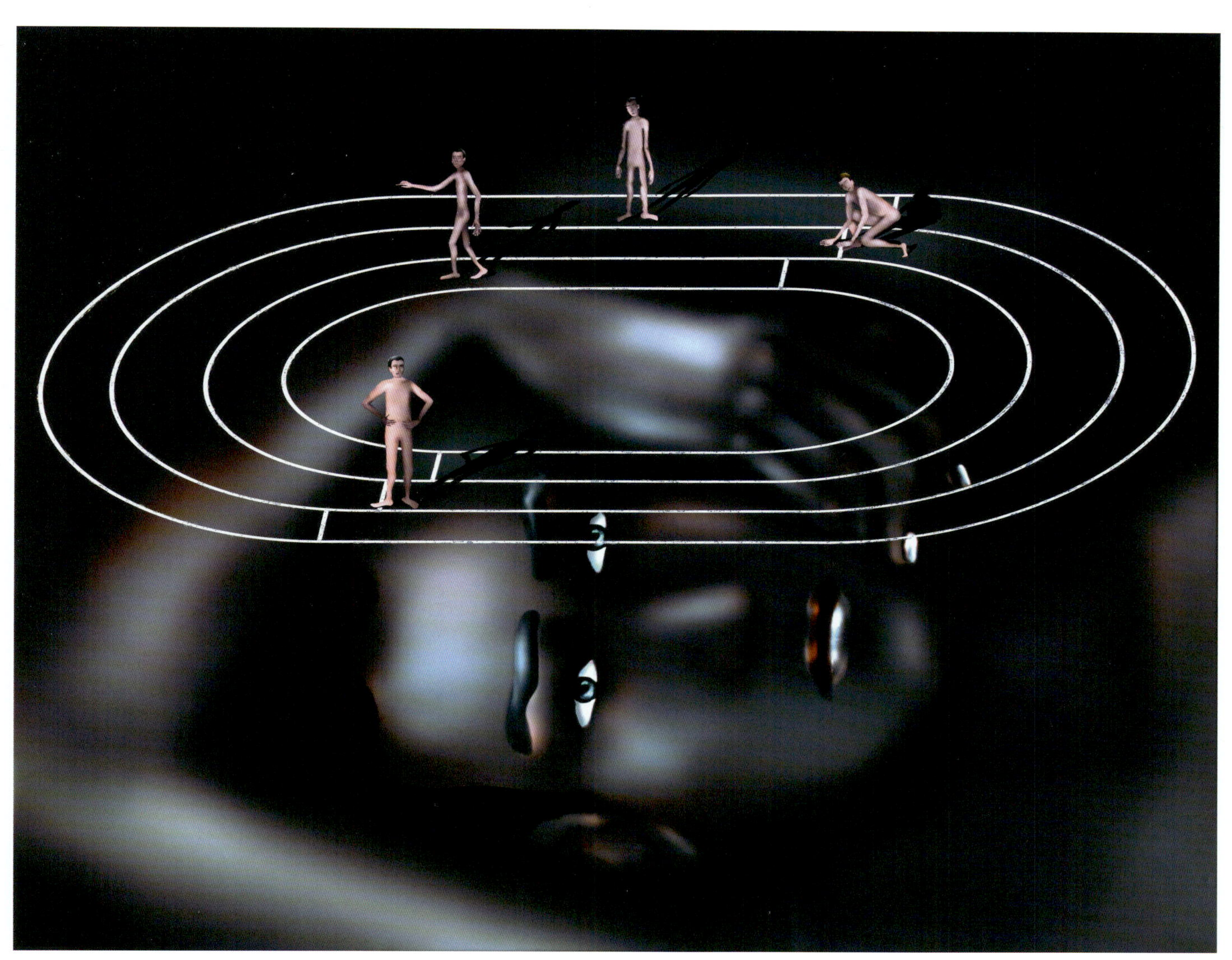

17   *Vicious Circles*, 2017

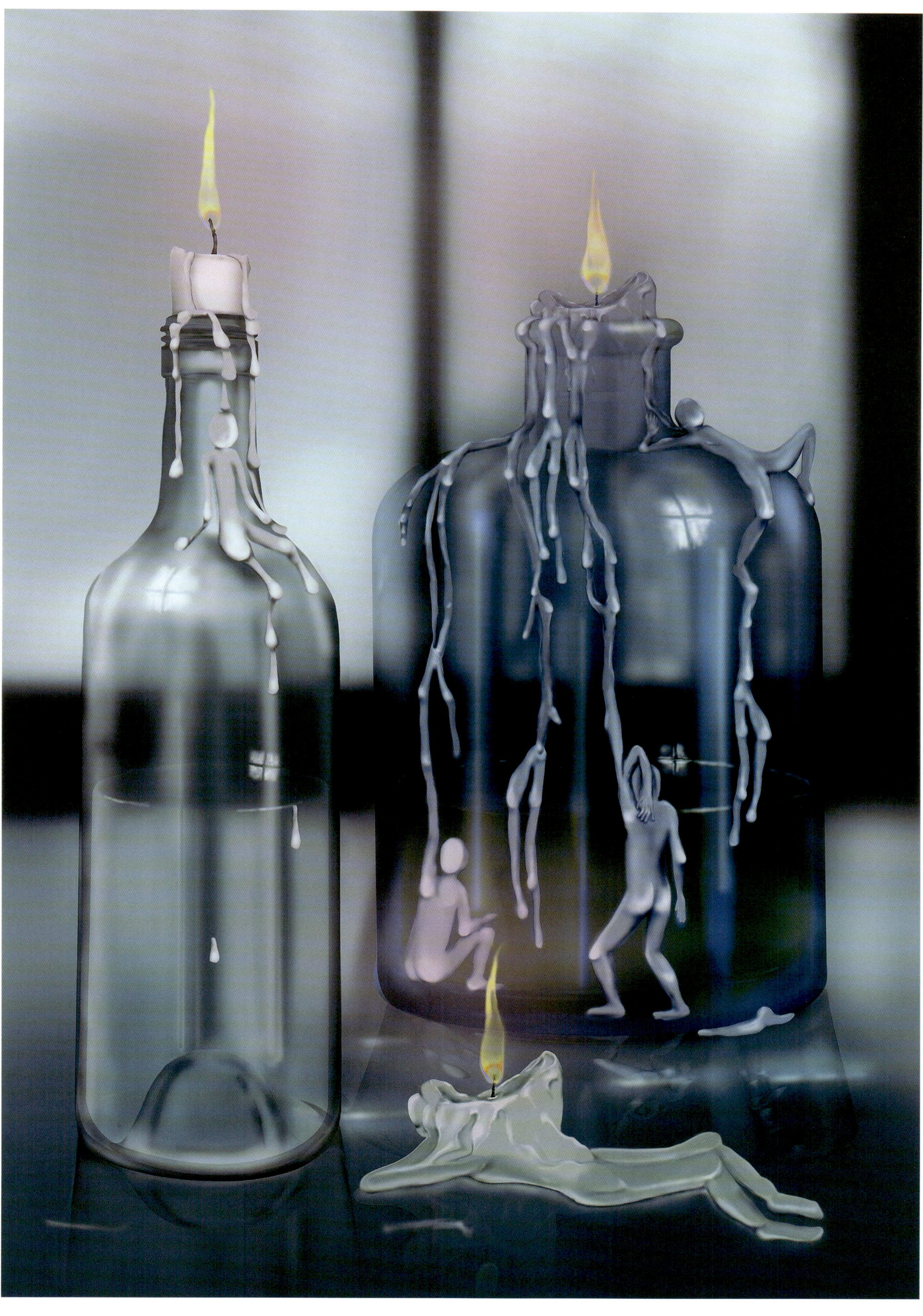

     Blue Tan, 2019

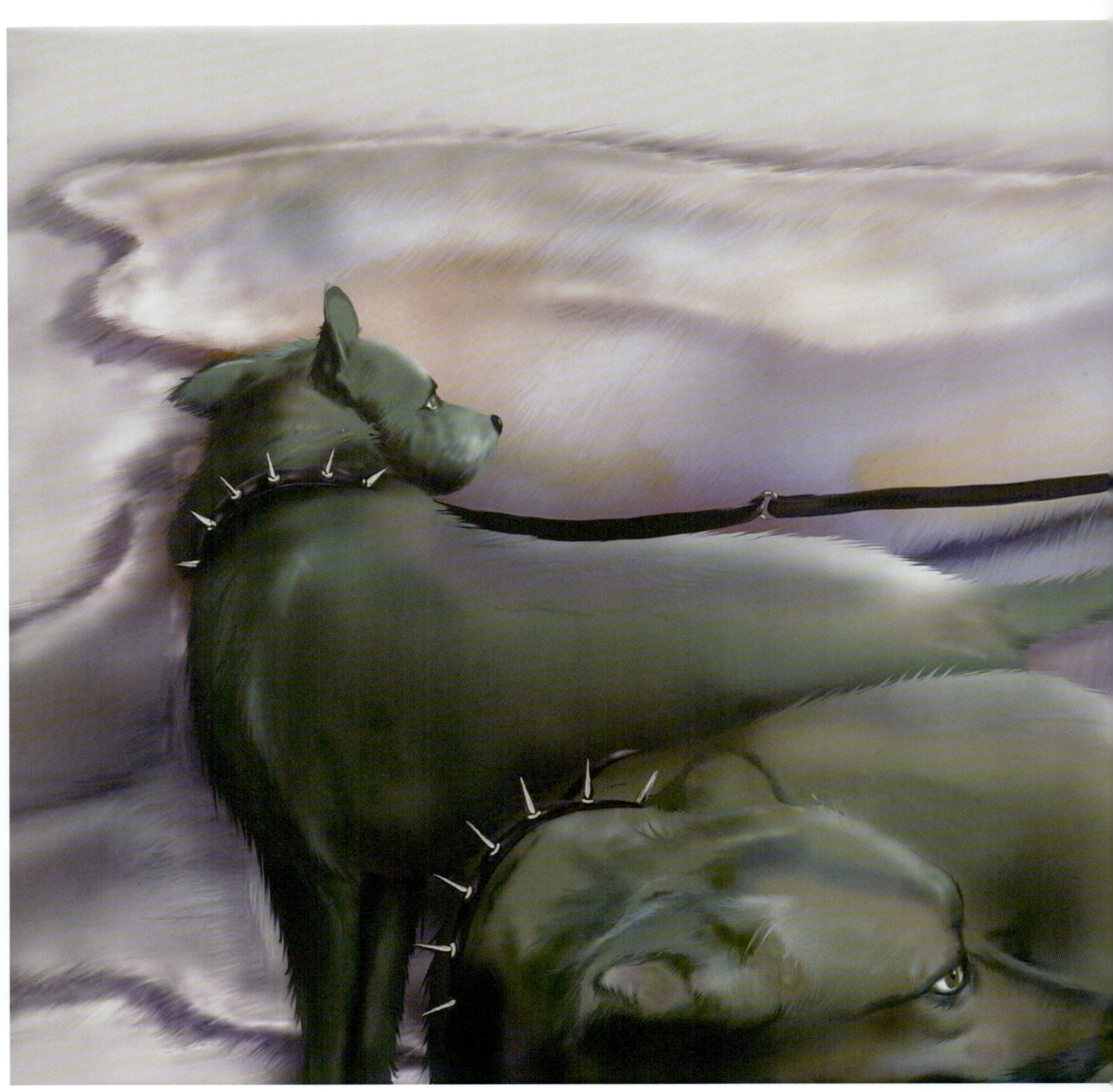

  Permission, 2021

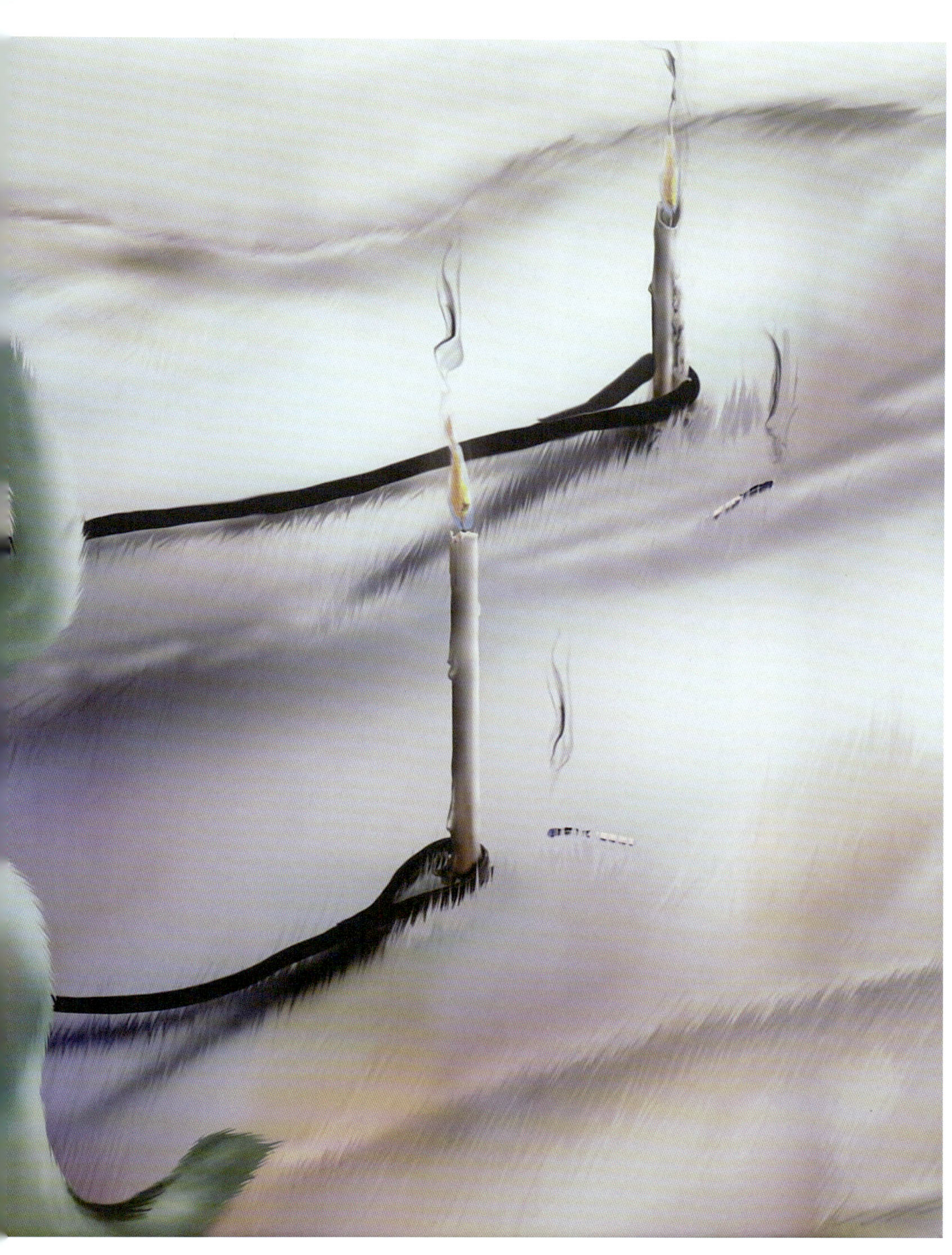

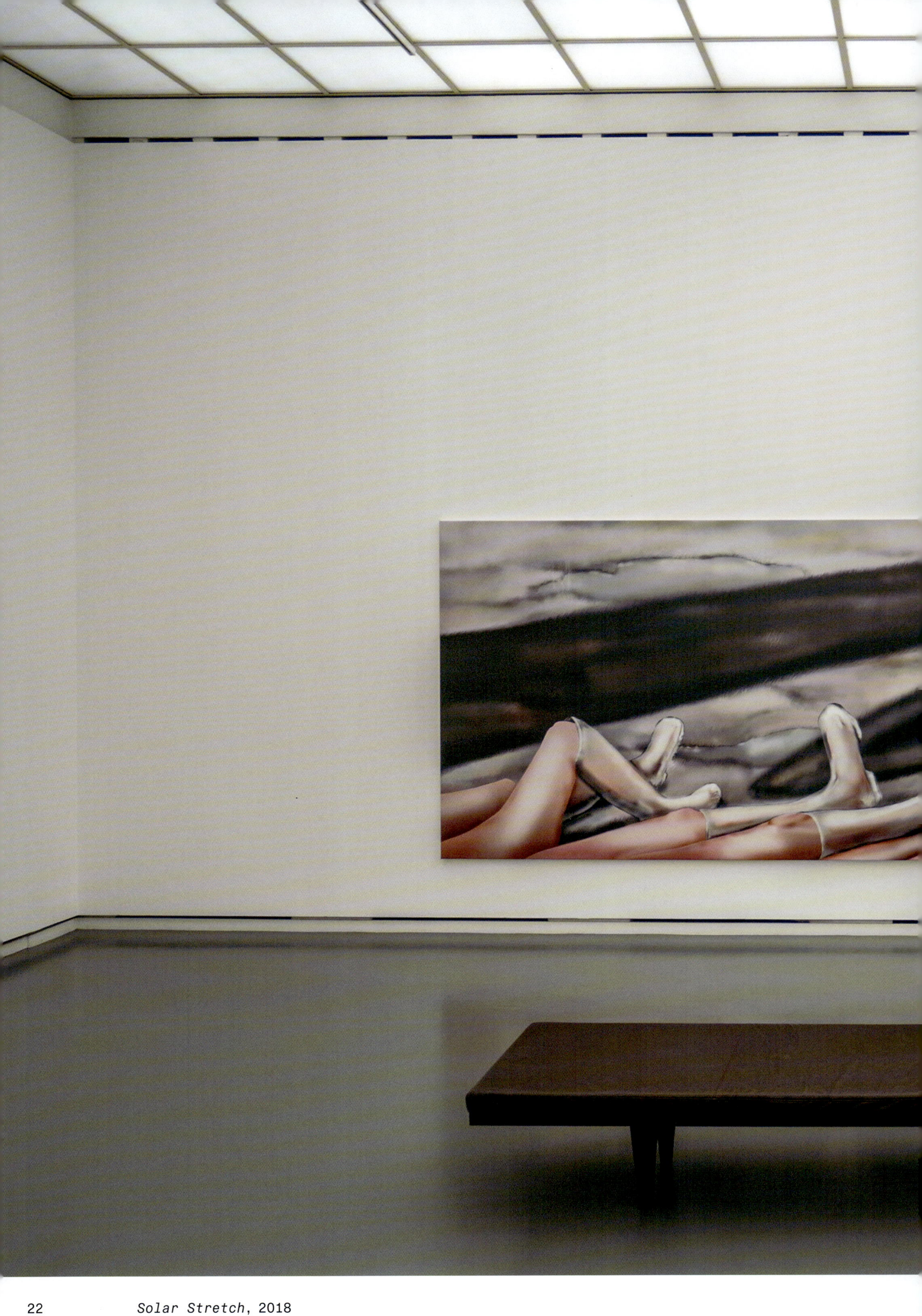

22   *Solar Stretch*, 2018

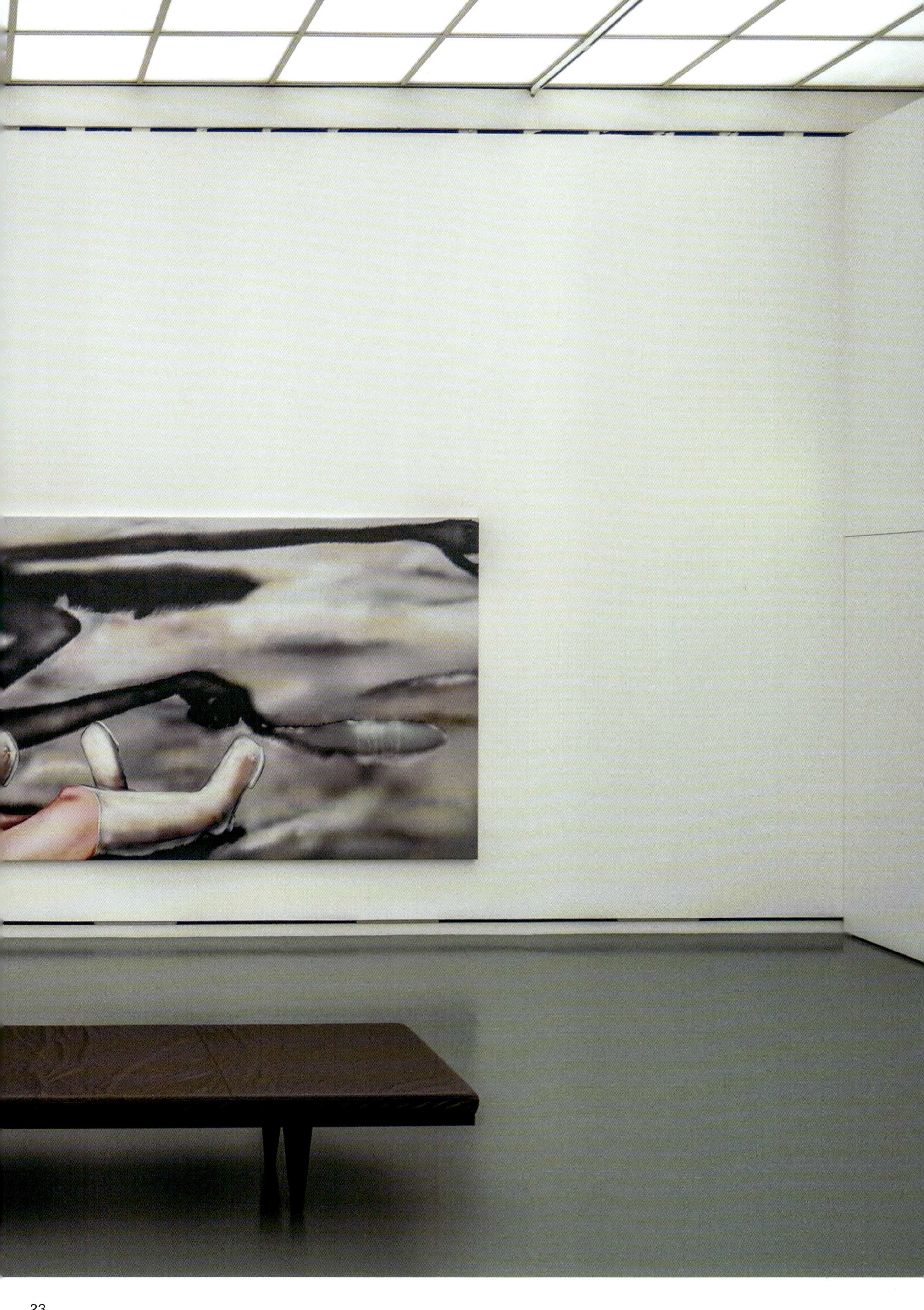

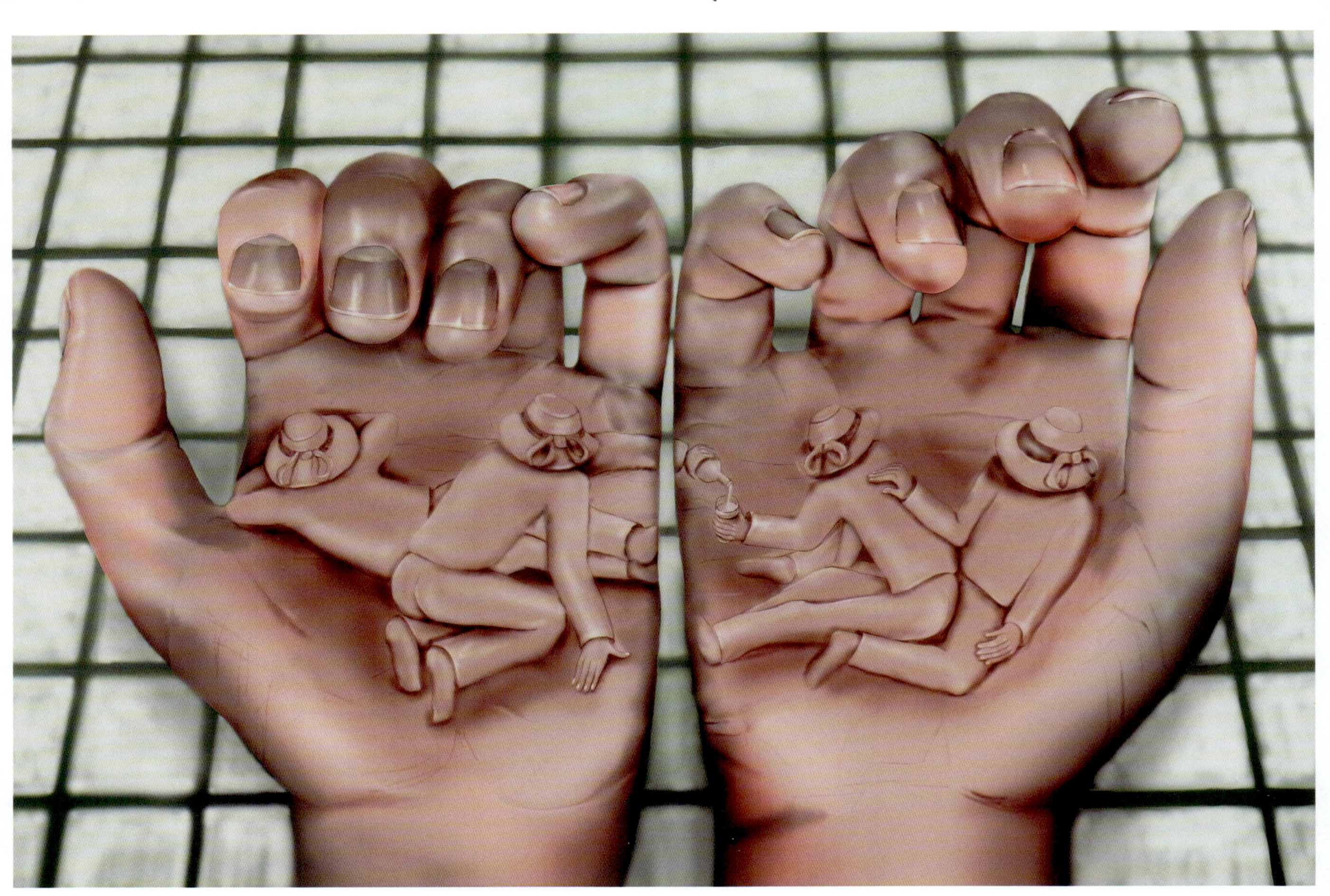

          Palm Reader, 2019

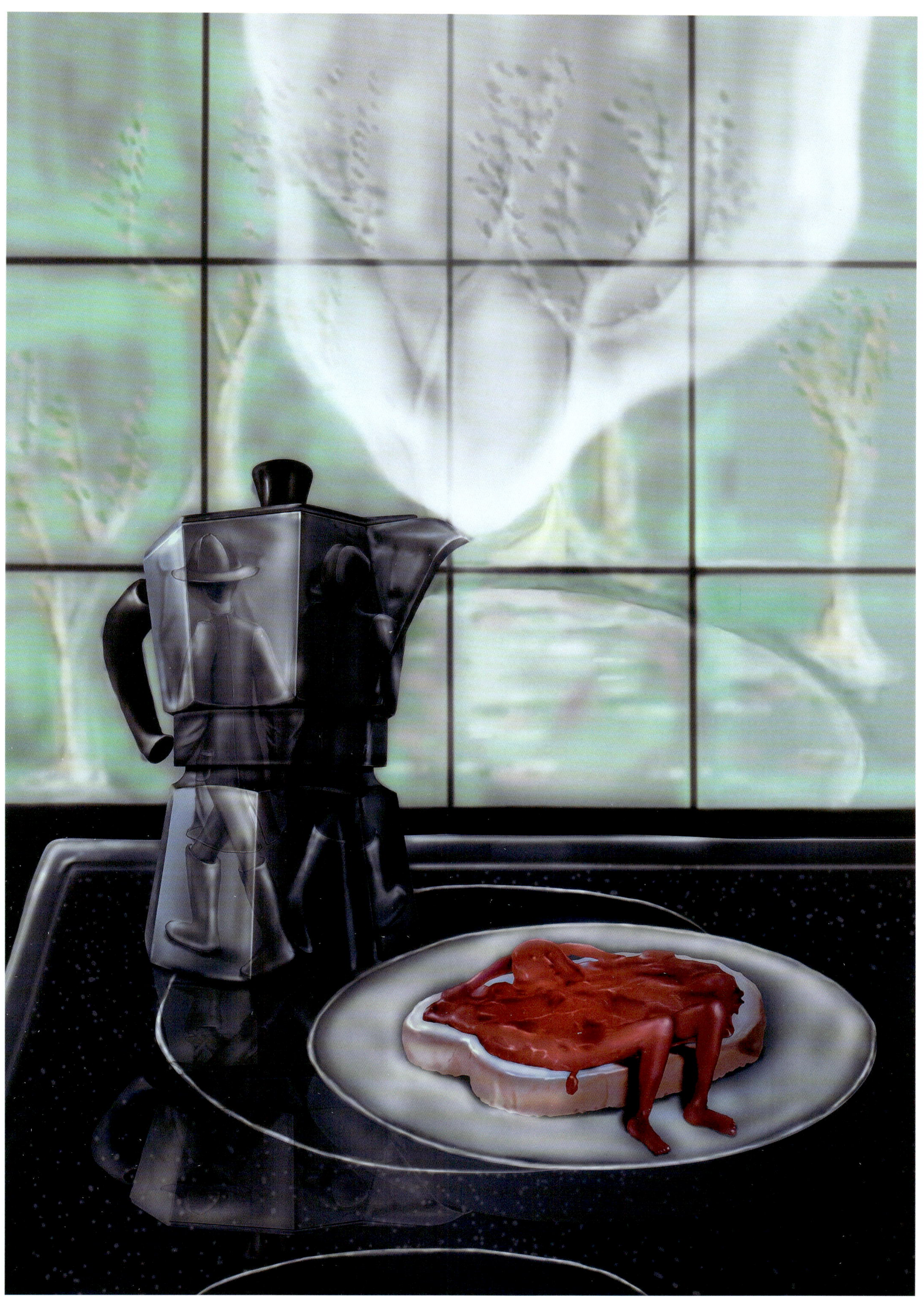

     Daily Jam, 2019

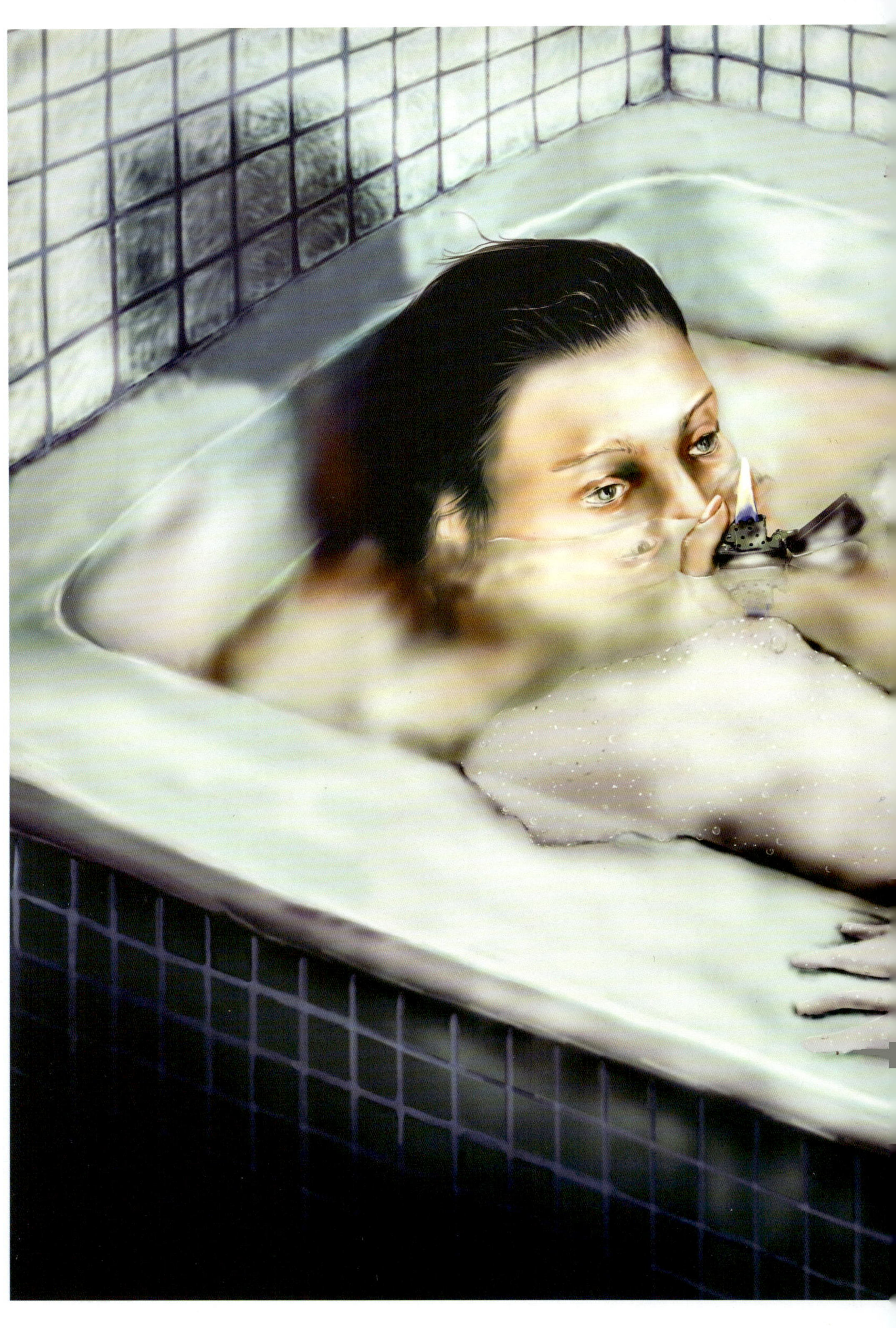

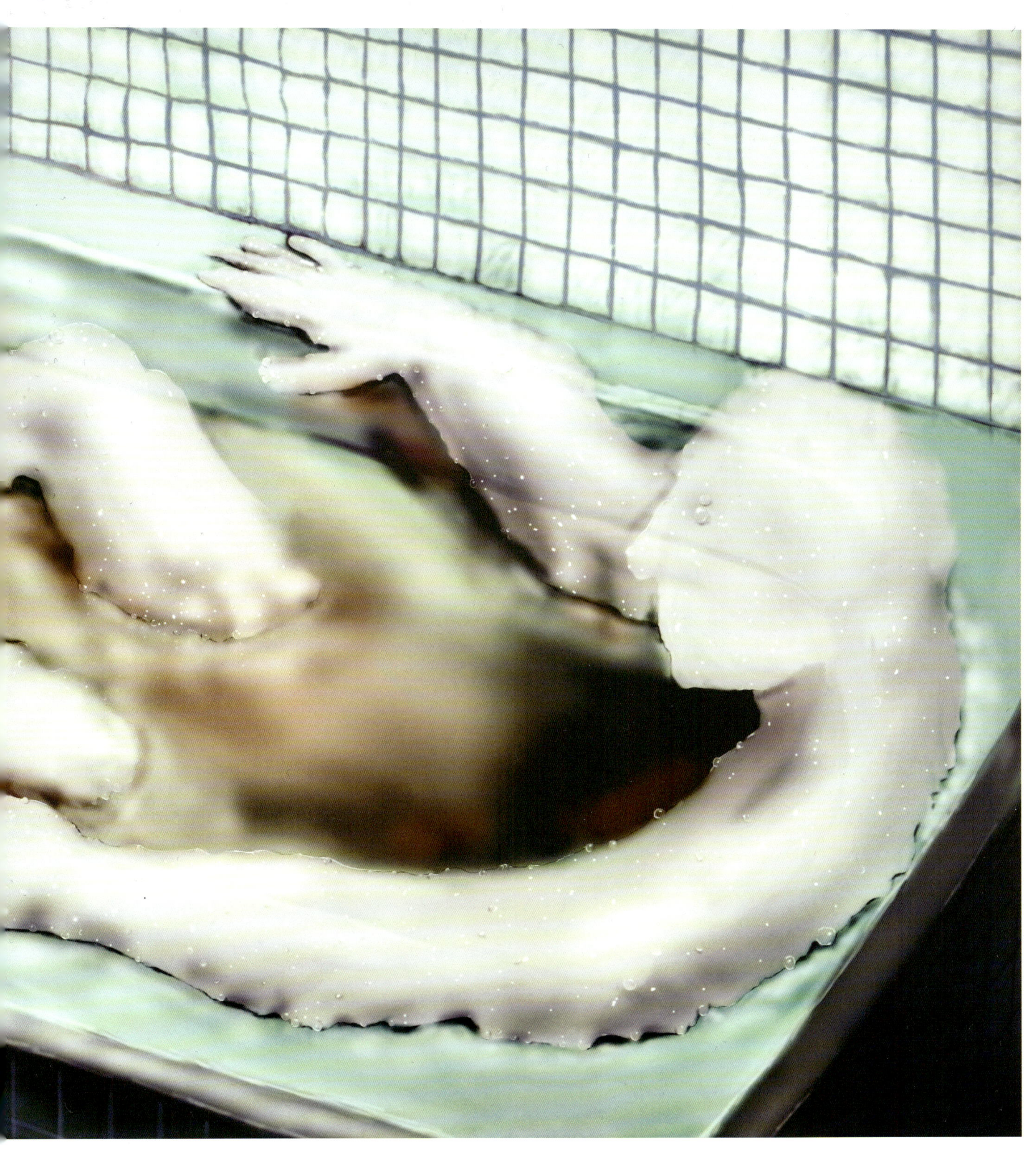

  Bubble Bath, 2020

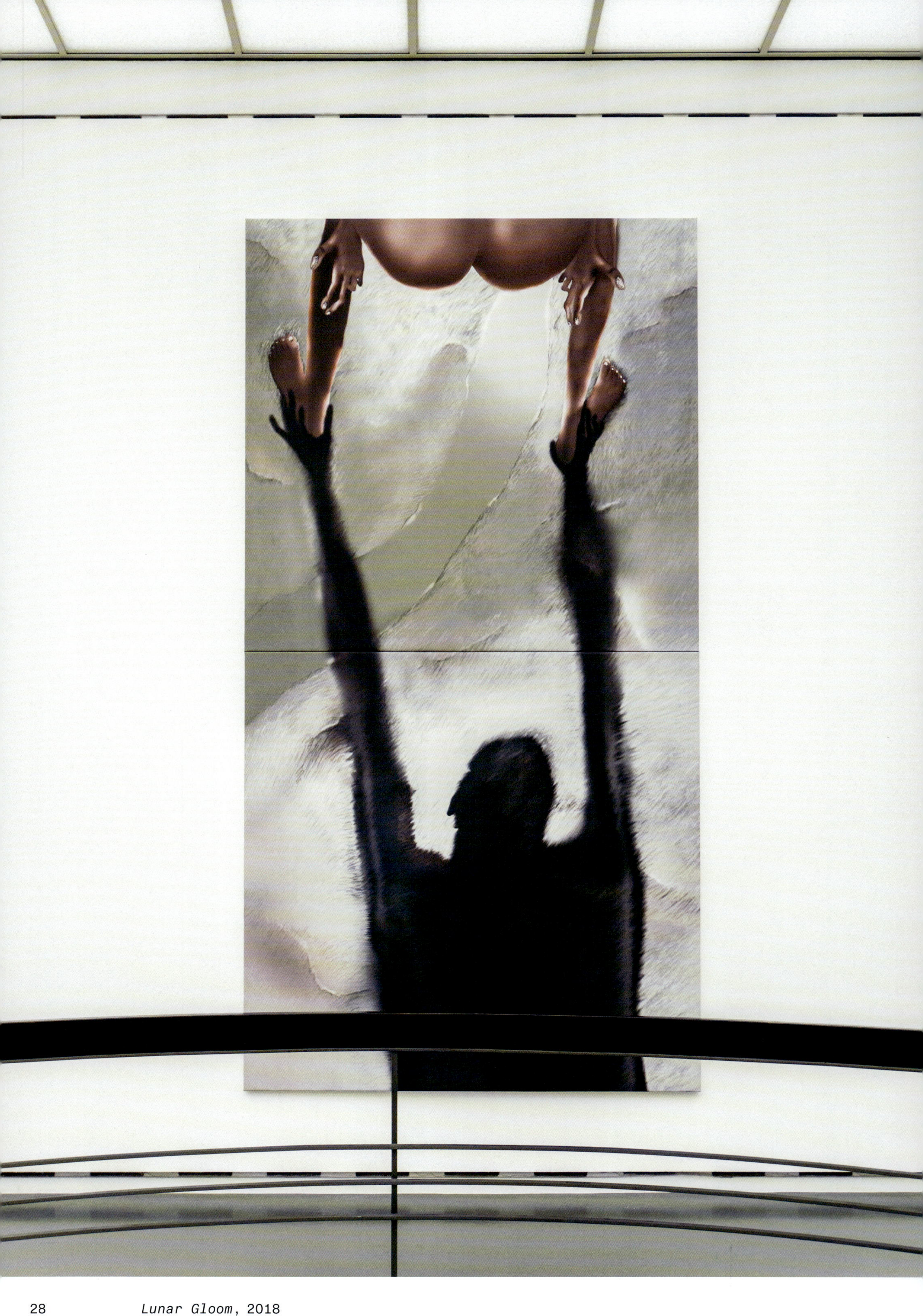

   Lunar Gloom, 2018

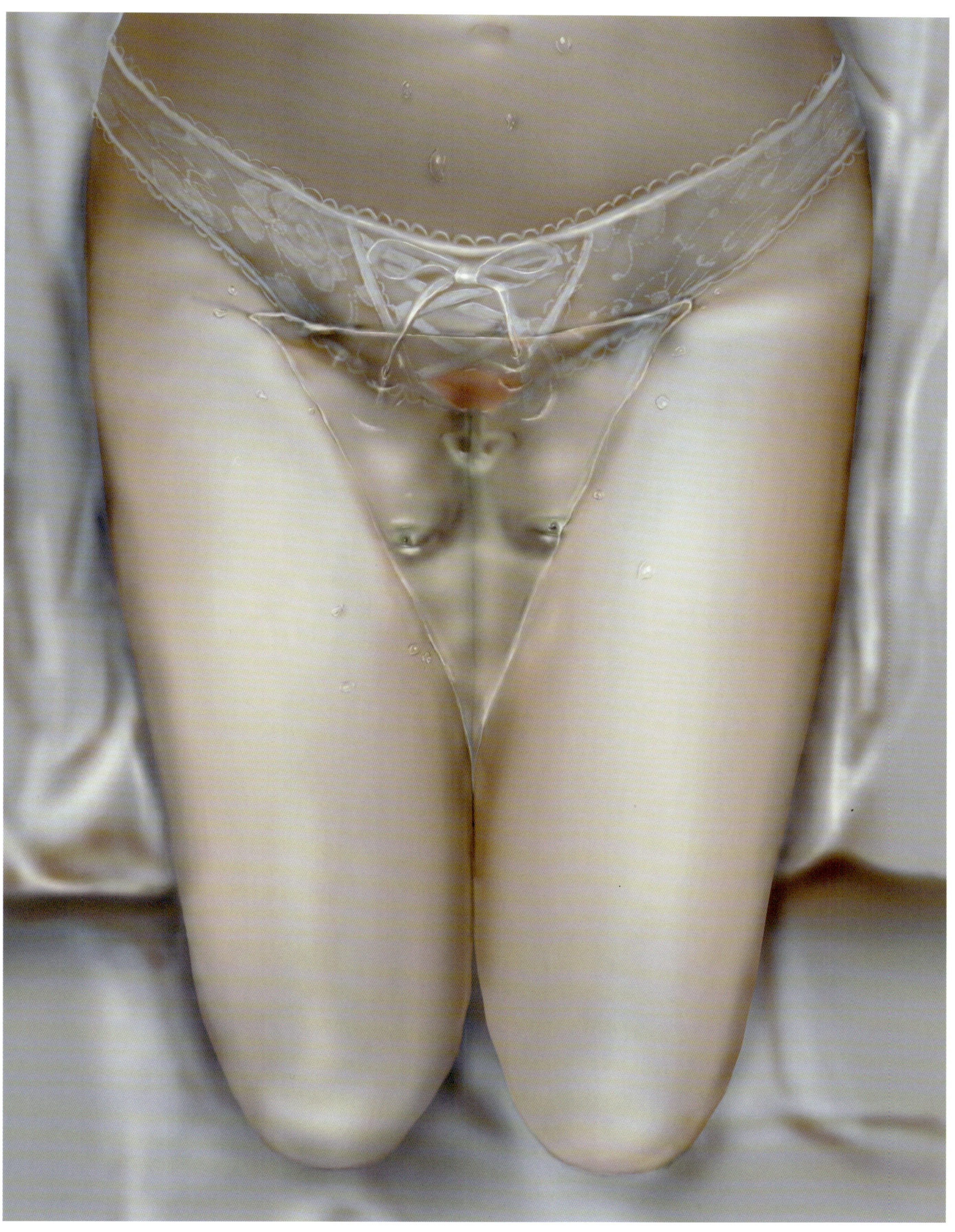

29   *La Piscine*, 2020

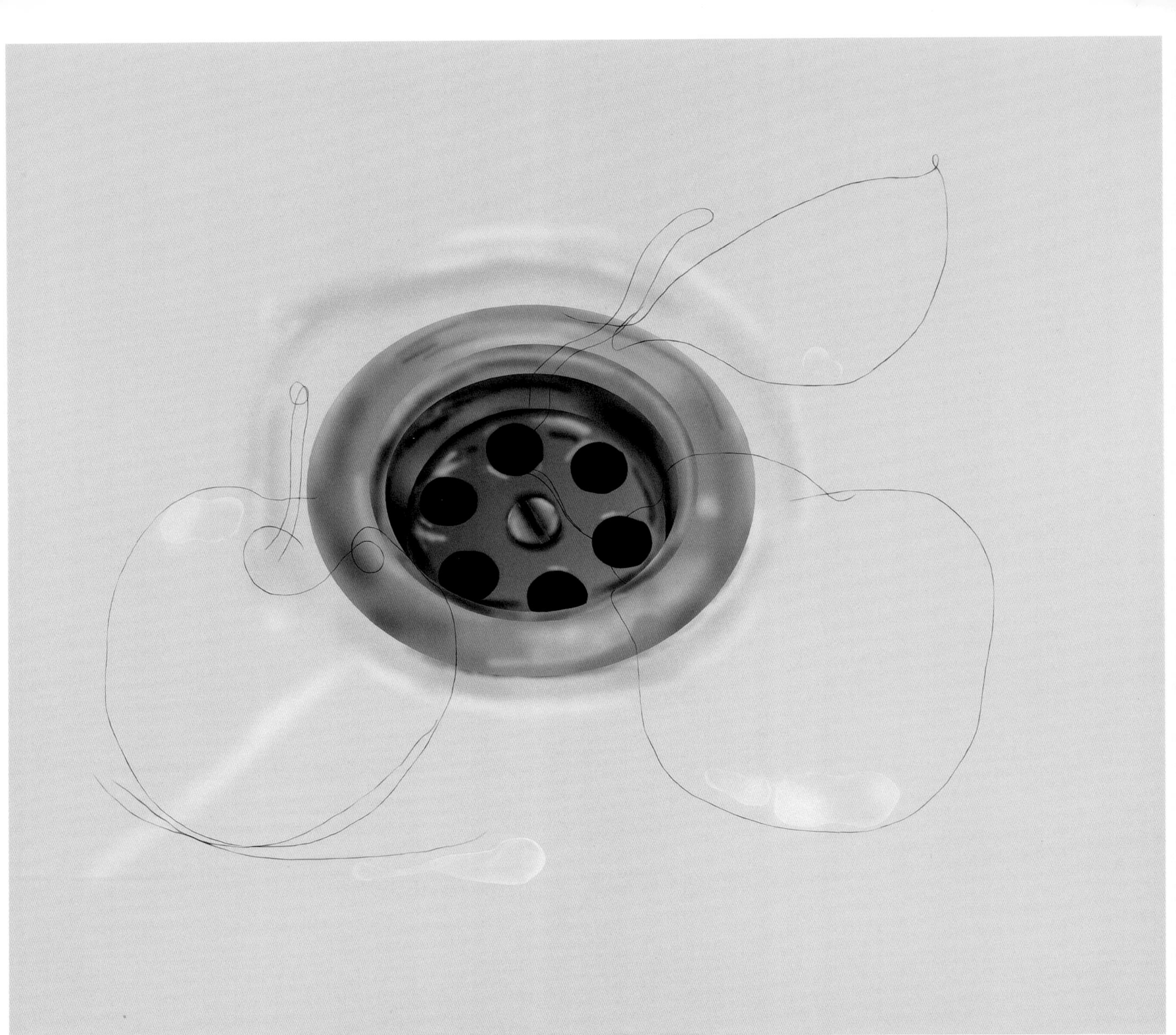

  Drained, 2019

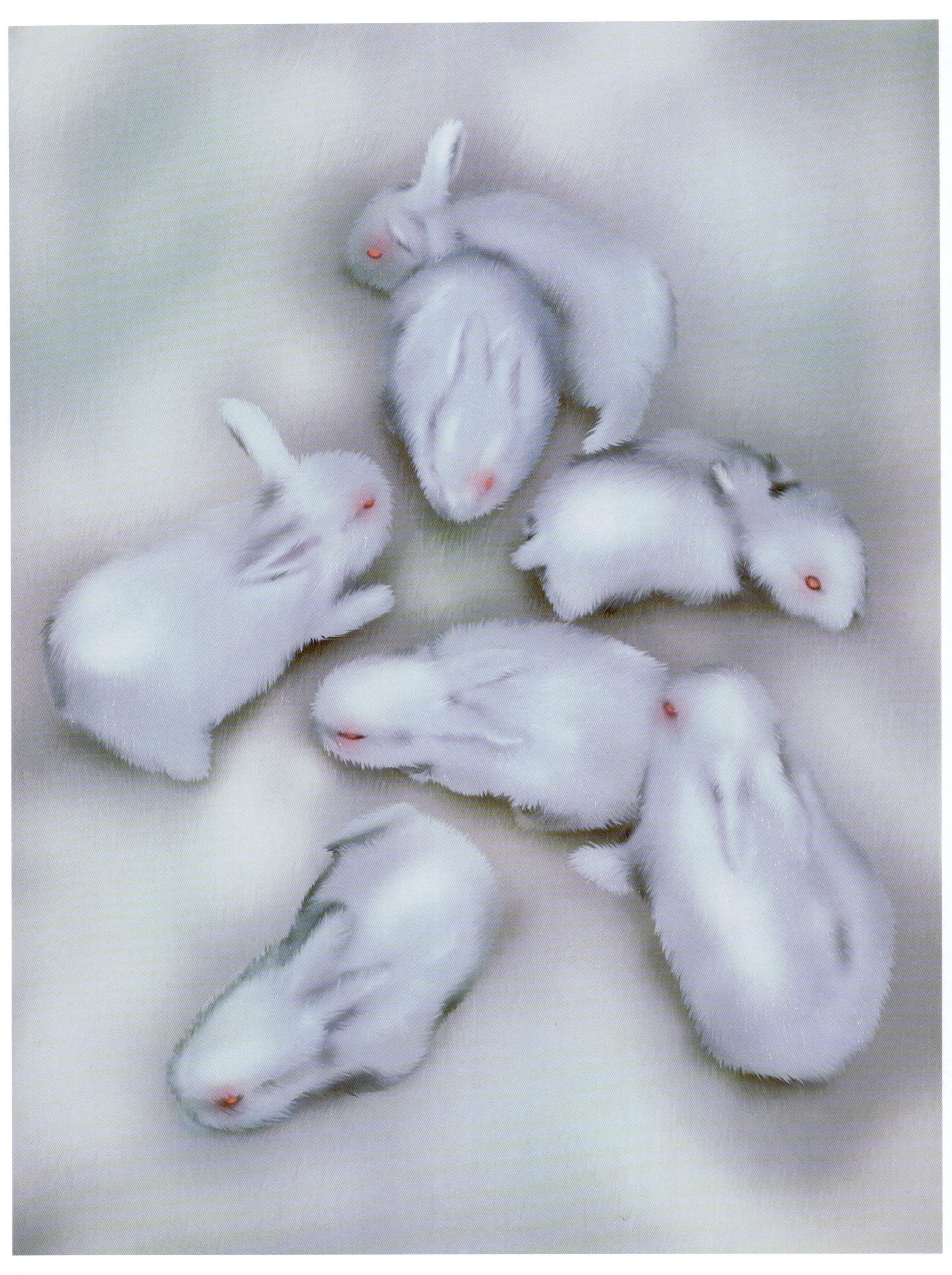

    Follow the White Rabbits, 2020

A SPECIFIC EYE, IN A SPECIFIC SHADOW, AT A SPECIFIC ANGLE

Your studio practice is partly similar to remote work. Do you paint in bed?

Sometimes, if I don't have much energy, but usually I come to the studio. I can really work from anywhere; I love working on planes and trains. When I don't have much time, when I know I have one hour to work, it can be worth three hours in the studio. The time constraint helps me make decisions, whereas if I had a full day, I would procrastinate it away.

If you think about Conceptual art in the 1970s, one of the reasons for its early international success was that an artist, let's say from New York, could travel with nothing to Europe and make a show that was much, much cheaper than a shipment of painting or sculpture. Your work doesn't really operate like that; you basically have two studios, a digital one you can carry with you where you do one half of the work, and a traditional physical one where you do the other half.

The beauty of my work is that the planning and the making can happen at the same time. You said half and half, but I think it's more like 80% on the computer, 20% in the studio. I can sketch my ideas as much as I can realize them, because with the computer I can change colors infinitely, format infinitely, alter composition infinitely. I borrow from one painting to the next quite easily, so I can conceptualize a whole show in the same space and the same manner as I am actually producing it. Once the image is ready, I print it and then the physicality of it emerges. I return to the studio where I add the final gestures, different gels or nail polish, latex or glitter, things like that.

When I'm painting there is always this object mediating between my body and the canvas. You don't use a paint brush, so what do you use?

It is literally just a mouse. I have tried a tablet where you can actually draw as you would with a pen or a brush: it became too direct. The mouse creates more of a distance. The trackpad is too clumsy and the tablet too gestural, whereas the mouse has a good balance between the two. Of course there is always my signature to it, but it is more the technique than my actual wrist movement. I think this is why I keep the mouse; there is something very controlled with it that in certain ways doesn't allow me too many liberties.

In other parts of your practice you have coded an idea of the signature into the work. You are removed, but also somehow present. Your actual fingerprint was blown up in *Late in the Game* (2021). In what other ways do you hide yourself within the paintings?

For all of them I add this last layer of gel medium that is made by my hand with a paint brush. This is the signature of the artist, which I am actually quite attached to. Unconsciously, this universe I'm creating has my own patina, including personal reference images. For example, my partner will be in some way in a lot of paintings, as I photograph him for more anatomically difficult angles.

I think a big part of the impact the paintings have is that they come from a screen and they initially look like a screen, especially when viewed in reproduction. In person, though, when you move around them, different materials reflect light and confuse the atmosphere of the surface. How much of that do you do live after you have printed the painting out, and how much is done anticipatorily on the computer?

Every time I think, "Oh my god I should plan this more." But each time I try to do that it confuses me while I'm painting on the computer. If I work with another material, like aluminum or mirror, then I have to think about this because the material takes on more importance. Also, the formats of the paintings are quite big, and I work on my laptop, which is much smaller, so they really become something quite different in the studio. A surface that I kind of ignored, or didn't realize was as beautiful as it was, suddenly becomes more off the computer when I have it as a physical object.

You can't fake it.

Exactly. Sometimes it's a surprise and sometimes it needs to be trashed and redone.

Over the last few years the compositions of your works have suggested a moment of action even though there is a relative feeling of calm within them.

Yes, there is always this passivity from them, but either some event or moment has just happened, or is about to. I'm looking for moments of fragility verging on chaos.

In 2020 Agata Pyzik, reviewing your exhibition at Dawid Radziszewski Gallery for *Artforum*, suggested that your works are depictions of a future. I'm not sure I ever pictured them that way. Sometimes when an artist is working with current technology, we tend to fantasize that they are working ahead of our time.

I guess they are past, present, and maybe future. There are a lot of references. Portraiture is something that has been done and redone forever. There is a reference to the past. There is a lot of the present as well, with the light of the screen, this artificial lighting. A lot of the figures that populate my paintings are sorts of avatars: they are no one and everyone, that is what I like about them. They are like a vessel to project oneself into. We have a tendency to think that technology is the future, but technology is now. The way my paintings are being done is something that is new, but it is very present too.

Anytime humans depict a future there is a certain optimism at play. The idea that we, as a species and civilization, could make it five more years, 50, a million. While your work can be quite dark visually—it can be sort of moody—there is still this sense of optimism within them. Maybe it goes back to the idea you mentioned of the avatar. The freedom to picture oneself as one would want.

It is a double interpretation; even for myself I'm not sure I am hopeful for the future. Sure, technology allows me to have some control over my image or connects me with people in a certain way. Maybe it gives me more freedom, but really at the end of the day I still need to go out into the world and have facetime and physically do the things in order for them to be real. Maybe soon the metaverse will take over and we can just live alone in a basement. I think it would be awesome, personally, and also terrifying.

One of the aspects that makes the work brilliant, visually and conceptually, is the way it exists physically in our world. This includes how you manage to capture that backlit feeling with color, which is not easy. Things on screens don't look like things on canvas or on PVC, but you pull it off. What would happen to your work in the metaverse?

I have to say I continue to have this fetish and fantasy for the actual painting, the hours that go into it, and the materiality and preciousness. I try to recreate it with a computer-assisted process and I would be sad to lose the materiality existing IRL.

I think it is good you bring up how the work is painting—it is painterly. One of the novelties for the audience when you began exhibiting was that the work didn't look like a painting. I'm interested in the way that some of the most interesting paintings done by our generation, yours included, take on a kind of vernacular visual form and then twist it toward a high form. Those original SketchUp assisted works by Avery Singer, Ebecho Muslimova's graphic cartoon line, Jamian Juliano-Villani and her meme aesthetics. In your work this vernacular form comes from graphic design, which you did for a living after having graduated from ECAL, Lausanne. Why do you think this feels so special and contemporary to the world right now?

Painting is a classic and has been done forever, and there was this idea for a long time that it could not be reinvented. I find it interesting that we have all found a new direction that can be brought to it. For me it is still painting because my process is really the same, except that I have the ability now to sketch and paint simultaneously on the screen. At the end of the day, the rendering is light and form and colors and shadows, etc. When you talk about graphic design, where I come from, it informs my work a lot, especially my formats. My instinct is always to go for a DIN format, like a poster. It's a format I have tamed. I can work so easily with it, and when I initially conceive a painting, it is always in that format, and I have to fight against that in order to change it.

One of the criticisms of your work, and that of these other artists I mentioned, is that it is vulgar in a formal sense. It can be confusing

          Mitchell Anderson   Louisa Gagliardi

to conservative viewers; the surfaces of your paintings are plastic not canvas, it is trashy, and does not show physical brushstrokes except where another medium is applied. Liminal states can be very exciting and upsetting for people to witness. Did you know this would be the case when you began working like this?

Yes, absolutely. The thing I was sure of was that I didn't want to fool anyone into thinking it was a conventional painting. For example, using an airbrush to reproduce what I already produced on the screen. It was a big conversation: what surface am I going to print on? The first instinct was to do it on canvas and I really didn't like it because it was too bleak, too powdery, and going in a too-obvious direction that wasn't even a wink toward painting. I thought of that PVC, banner-like material, that, first of all, had a shine, this silky, almost skin-like glow to it, that I love. It has this pure flatness to it that reminds me of the screen. The second conversation was whether it should be framed; people wanted to hide the sides. If you look at the sides of the paintings it is clear that it is a print. That is what is interesting about it, otherwise I would learn how to airbrush or whatever, but then it would not have the same flatness, and it wouldn't make any conceptual sense, because I would still have to do the whole process on the computer before using another technique.

I can see the prints around the studio, and they are beautiful before you go in and add the gestural marks. How do you find the courage to change the surface when you don't know if it will work?

The beauty of it is that the first part of the process, the print, I can fail on. I can do it and redo it and try again until it's perfect. That is the same as the computer, there isn't a big risk. If I don't like it, there can be multiple versions until I get to the one that becomes a work. Sometimes I have a first idea of what I can add onto it and it will be terrible, so I can have another printed and redo it. I have a lot of freedom to arrive at the final product.

Before current printing technology, for hundreds of years it was impossible to freeze one stage of your painting and experiment freely until you wished to move on. Maybe this was what Hercules Segers was getting at in the 17th century.[1] You have a potentiality here, both on the screen and the studio, that feels extremely contemporary, similar to your use of reflections. Has it always been true that the viewer relates to the figures in your works through glass, water, inky shadows? Where does that interest come from?

I think I am unconsciously attracted to shiny surfaces. You referred to me in a text once as a magpie, which I really hadn't thought about before, but it is an attraction I have. It also relates as a reference to the screen and the light it gives. It is about how one curates oneself in the world and how the image goes through a filter, or a surface or a screen, and that feels like a protection for the self, the way makeup can be.

This is where a criticality enters your work, it's like Jacques Lacan and his mirror stage, the idea that we can be self-objectifying. When that theory was formed 90 years ago, that objectification could really only have happened through a mirror. The idea that the general populace now self-objectifies all the time seems very central to your work and the figures that populate it.

The work deals a lot with the subject of narcissism. The figures look at themselves or gaze at the viewer and themselves through a surface, one that reflects both ways. I think nowadays we desire to have so much control over appearances and who looks at us and who we want to look at. Even doing this interview live is kind of freaking me out, as I can't edit my words as much as I would like, for example if we did this by email. Algorithms might define a lot of what we look at, but we also create what we want to see in the world. One other thing that is quite important when you look at

          Mitchell Anderson   Louisa Gagliardi

one of my paintings is that you don't know who the voyeur is. Am I intruding into their universe or are they intruding into mine? Are they seeing through me? It depends how it is being looked at and who is looking at it.

There is a double generosity to the viewer. Physically, as they are made to be seen in person and unveil surface-level secrets as one moves around, but also intellectually the viewer is not sure where they stand. They can tend toward the kind of Vélasquez, *Las Meninas* (1656), set up. If we view all these figures as avatars —they could be any of us—could I also view them as self-portraits?

Of course I will project consciously, or not, something of mine or myself directly into them. I know where they actually come from. They are always a collage of a set of references. If it is a perspective that is complicated, like from low to high, I will take a photograph of someone. I am not an anatomy magician of any kind; this is why I use the computer. I might also want some type of obscure lighting, so I will use another painting and, in the end, maybe five reference images will be part of it, because I want, say, a specific eye, in a specific shadow, at a specific angle, etc.

When we think about the shift to modernism a century ago, we give partial credit to the camera because it provided the viewfinder, which allowed these compositions that we can't see with human binocular vision. All those paintings by Robert Delaunay of the Eiffel Tower were conceived because of this, Alexander Rodchenko's new forms, the photography of László Moholy-Nagy that then affected the constructed work. This idea of thinking about using Photoshop, as you do, as a vital tool that changes how an image is created and received is important. Some of the earliest pieces you made were specific portraits coming from iPhone shots, like the one of Pierre and Charles (*Pierre & Charles*, 2015, see p. 59), but you quickly took the works toward further surreality and complexity.

When I started to do those paintings I was, at the time, already doing commercial illustration on the computer, but it was much more angular, much more Fernand Léger-esque and, of course, they were illustrating something. I got bored of this, so I started to play around, and came up with a new language through an instinctive way of learning. The portrait, when one learns a new technique, seems like a go-to, of course, and if I'm being honest that is how it started. I wanted to try something new, so I got out photographs of friends on my phone. The common denominator was that they pictured social gatherings, with hands near faces, using them as a protection—smoking, biting their nails, drinking, whatever. As my technique improved it allowed me to zoom out; by becoming more realistic I could become more fictional. By learning my craft, I was able to expand my universe. I love storytelling; I don't want them to be illustrative, but I like that they are narrative.

There is a whole trajectory in recent art in the idea that you had a job to pay your bills and then, through a sense of boredom and glitching in the job you were meant to do, you made your break-through. It takes you toward a way of working and a visual style that is unique, coming not from art school, but from the real world. I'm thinking of Richard Prince, doing tear sheets for Time Inc., and Barbara Kruger as head designer for Conde Nast magazines, where they fool around on the company's time and they break out of these visual styles.

The best ideas may come out of boredom.

You cite art history. You steal from it as a background on which you collage. Who and why?

That is a really wide question. My go-to at the moment would be Caravaggio for lighting, and Rembrandt of course; for color I look at Lautrec a lot; I am a huge fan of Pierre Bonnard. For interactions

  Mitchell Anderson Louisa Gagliardi

and body positions there are a lot of Renaissance painting references. I love browsing big digitized archives like the one from the Metropolitan Museum collection. I will just go on there because I'm looking to draw a certain nose, or an eye, also how a fabric is being painted. You mentioned earlier that before we had photography it was difficult for us, as artists, to view something a certain way —I feel this is the same when I'm trying to render something; it is important for me to see a painting. If I look at your shirt, I can see it, but I need to see how it is painted in order to do it myself.

We live at a time of an overload of information, content, and technology. A couple hundred years ago if you wanted to be a painter you might pack up and go to Paris to study and visit the Louvre and then maybe head down to Florence and do the same thing with the Uffizi. What is amazing in our current moment is that there is a high level of access for many more people, and this happens online. You no longer have to be mildly wealthy to have simple visual access to these masterpieces. Your ability to collage and research and see simultaneously is only possible from this exact moment.

Well, absolutely. I think it also makes a lot of sense with the way that I do the work. Everything is redone but I do take from many sources and references to come up with my own vision.

If your work was an iPhone app would it be Instagram or Uber?

Either. I don't have much patience, and love instant gratification.

Grindr or the App Store?

Grindr, for sure. Ha ha! In this case, almost instant, and greater gratification …

Candy Crush or that calculator that teens use to hide their nudes from their parents?

I don't know it, but definitely that last one!

You never heard of that? It's like a calculator and you choose something like an equation or whatever, and when it is typed it opens up a hidden file system on the phone which is only accessible through this app. They are locked in there from prying parental eyes.

It would definitely be that one then. This idea of a hidden surface to show more is important to me and, in the paintings, there is the idea of an oncoming chaos that is reflected, the teens might not know it, but it is reflected in that app. It's a hidden chaos. In my work I paint a universe I want to project myself onto and into, to be both antisocial hermit and glamorous exhibitionist.

```
1        Hercules Segers (c. 1589-c. 1638)
was a Dutch painter and printmaker of the Dutch
Golden Age. He has been called "the most inspired,
experimental, and original landscapist" of his
period and was an even more innovative printmaker.
He is mainly known for his innovative etchings,
mostly of landscapes, that were often printed on
colored paper or cloth, with colored ink, hand-
colored, and often hand-cropped to different sizes.
He also made use of drypoint and a form of
aquatint, as well as other effects, such as running
coarse cloth through the press with the print,
for a mottled effect (from wikipedia.org/wiki/
Hercules_Seghers).
```

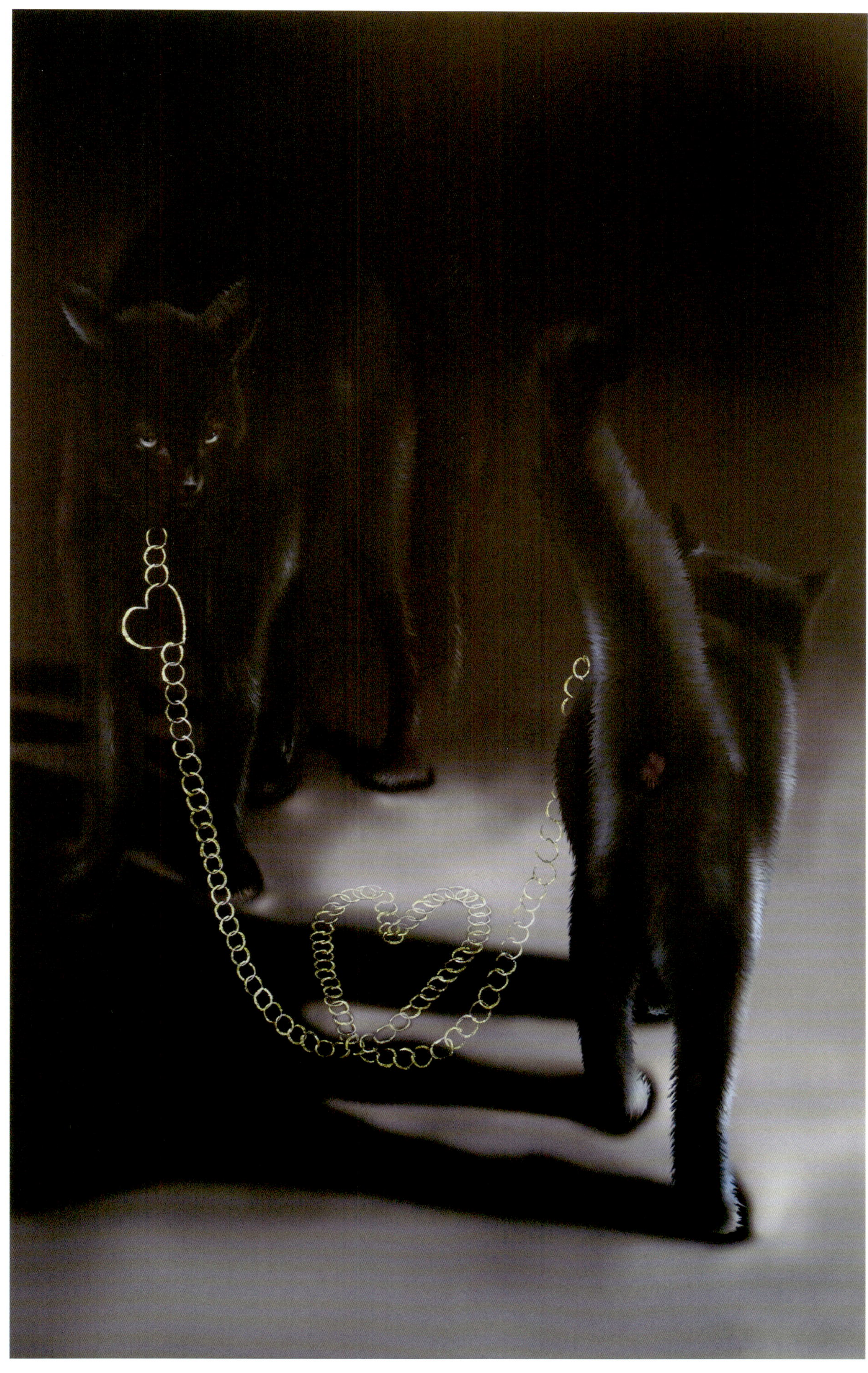

     Linked, 2019

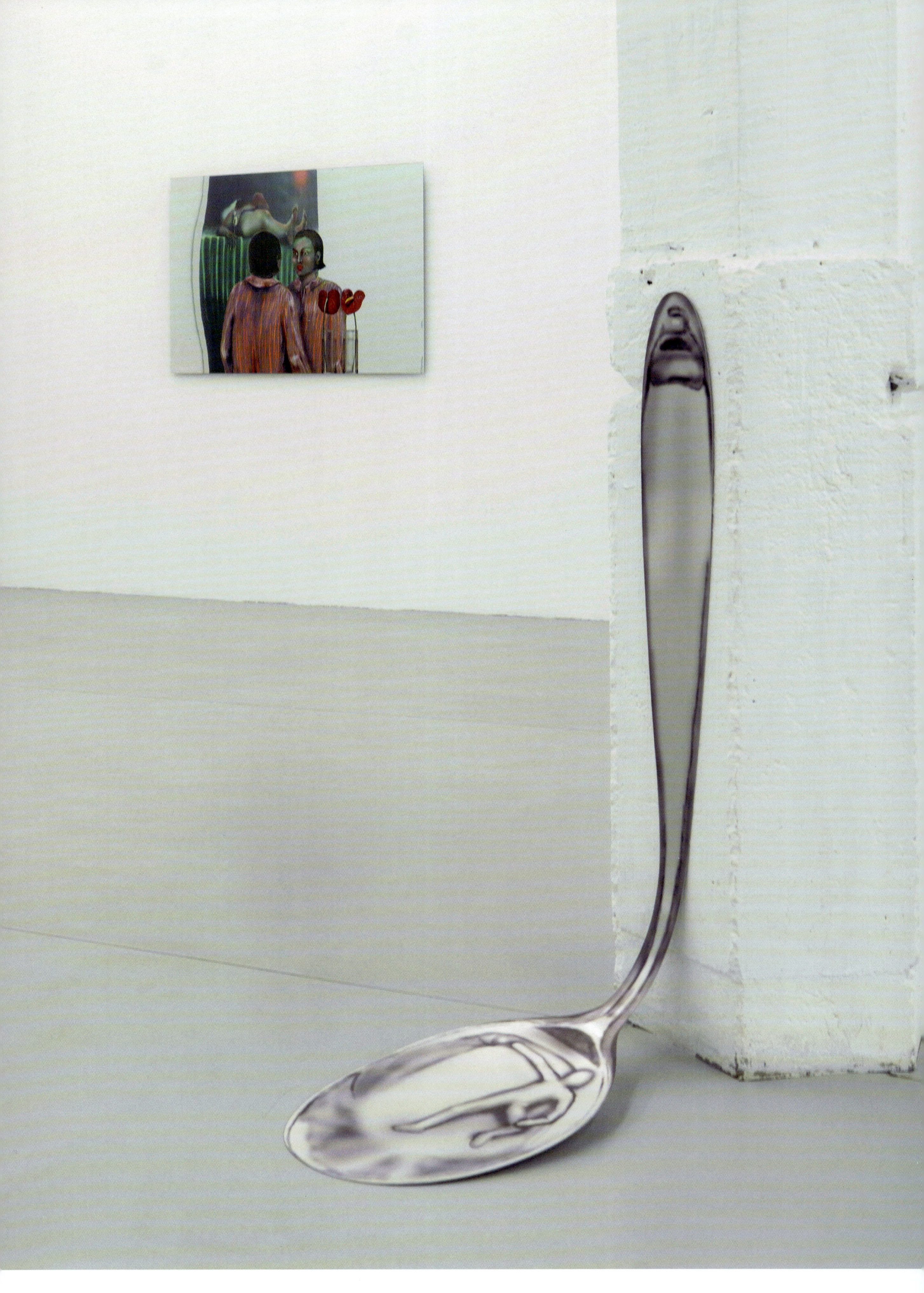

Mirror Mirror, 2020   *Spoon 1, 2020*

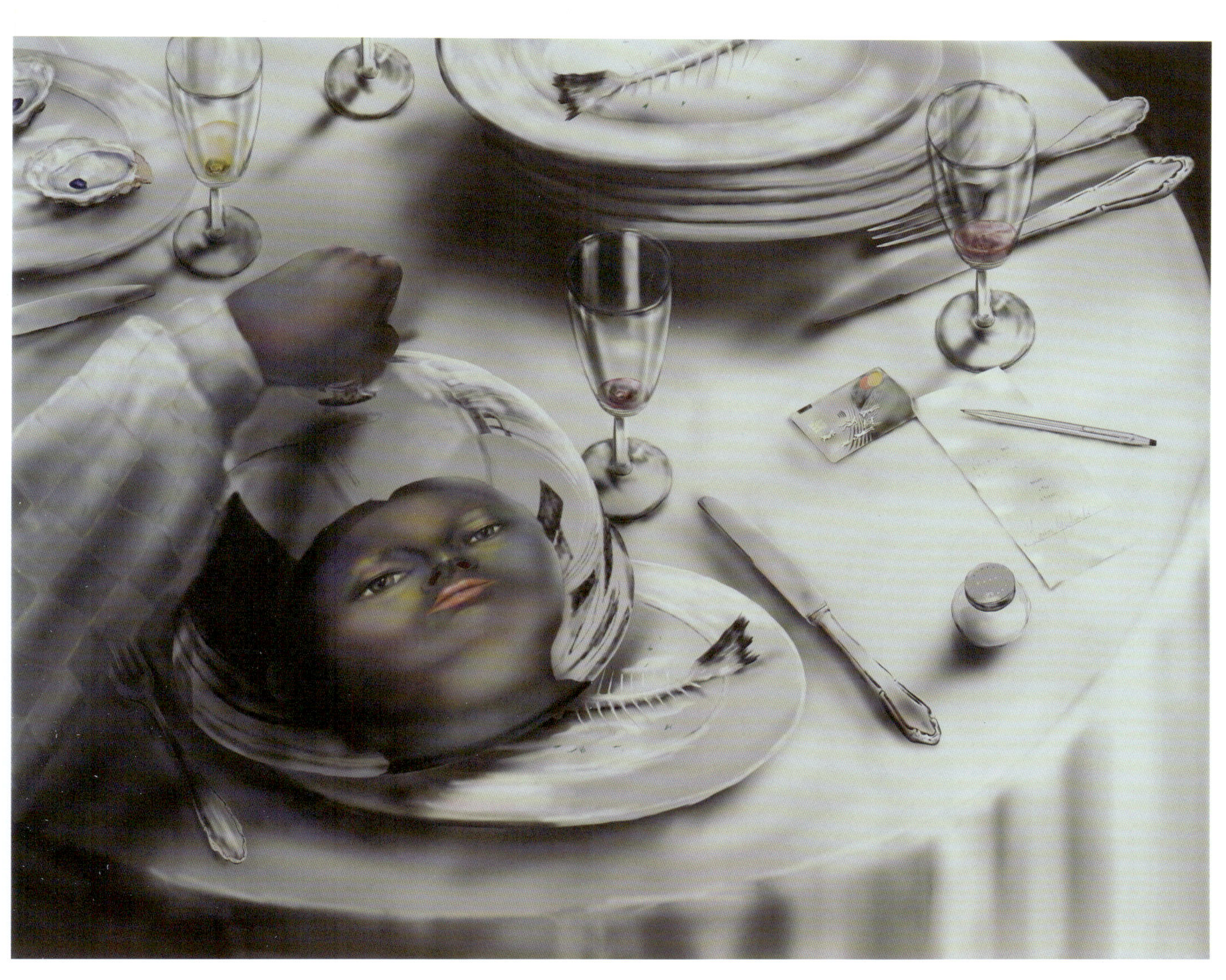

     Check Please, 2021

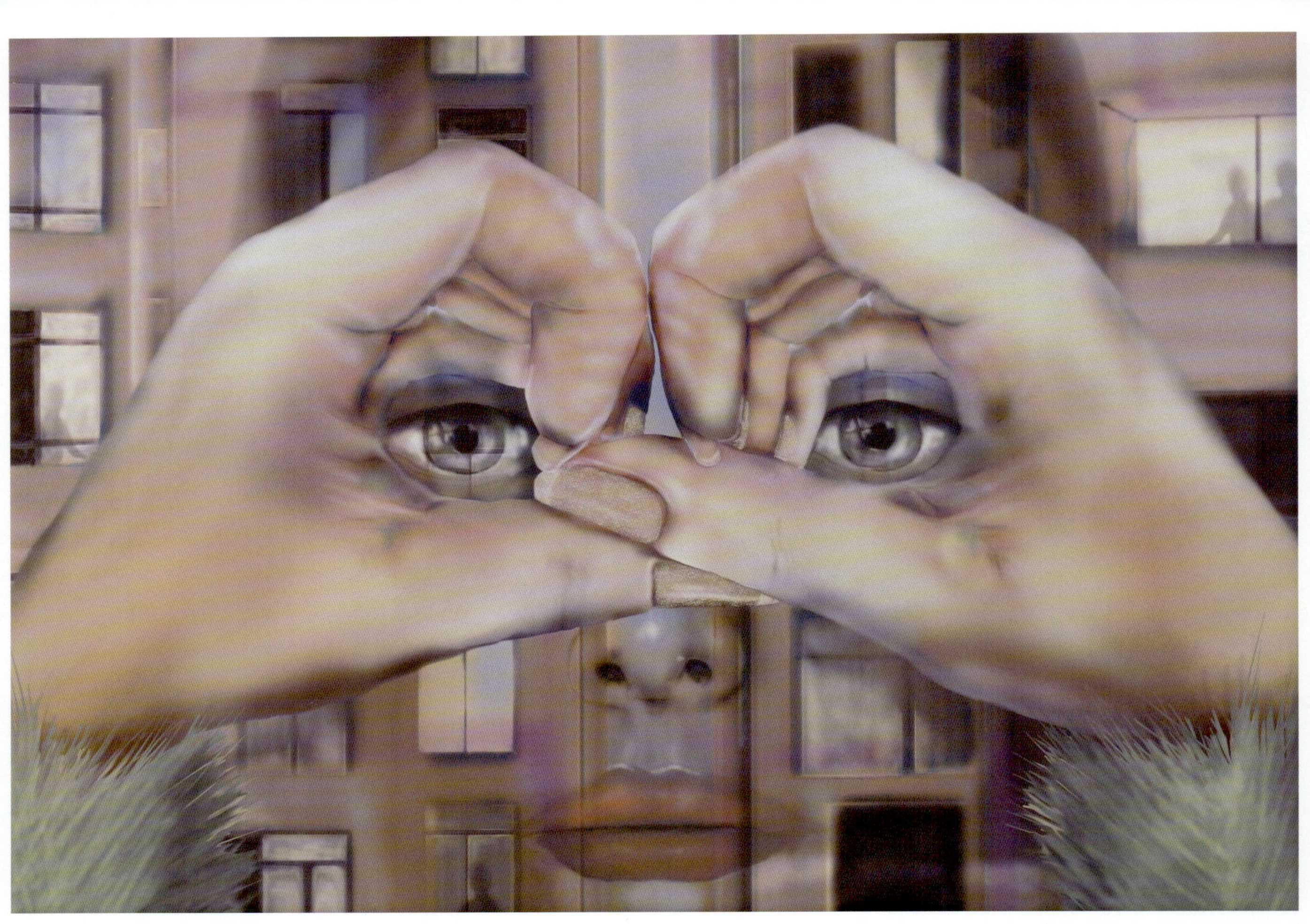

    Rear Window, 2021

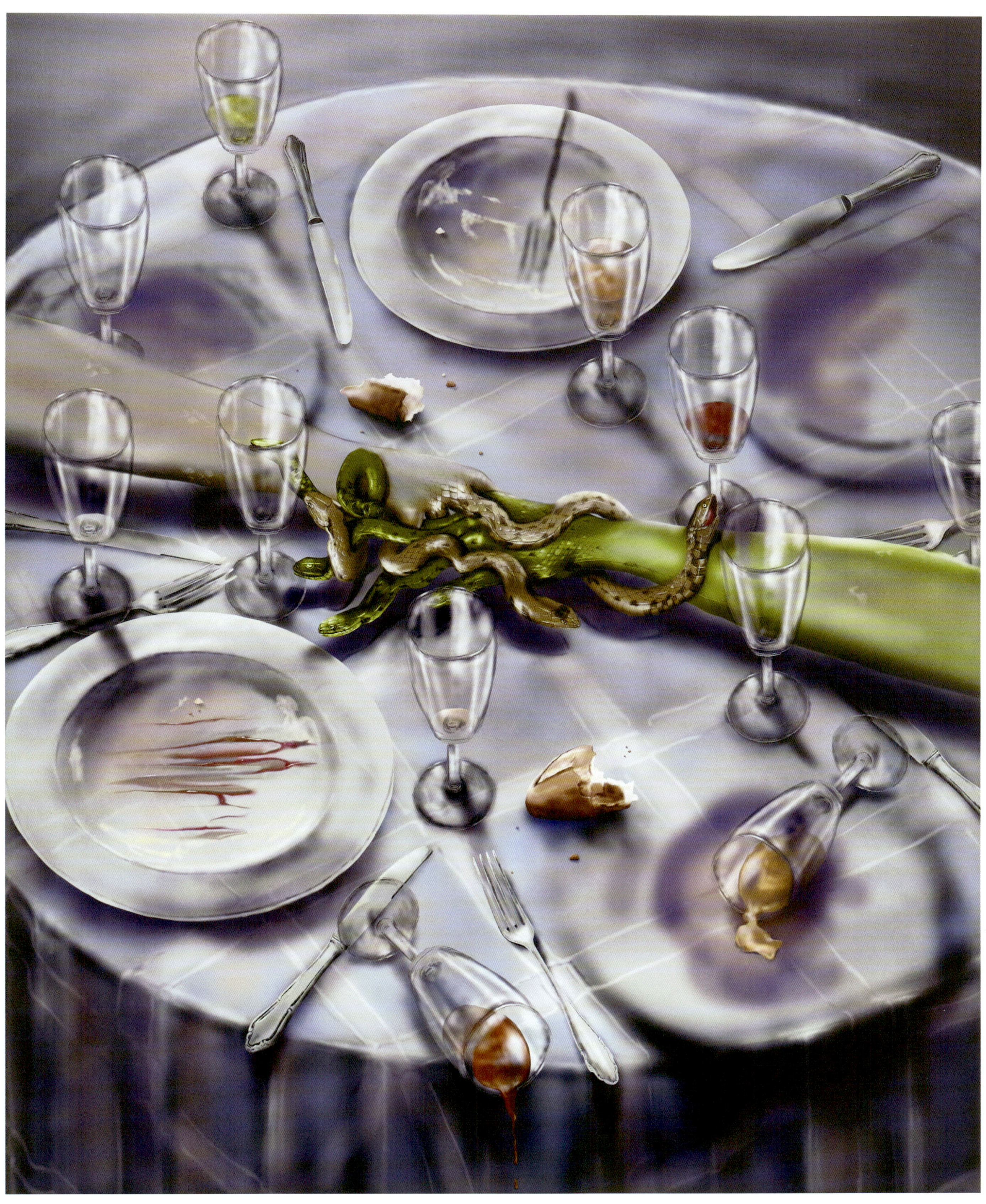

     Over the Table, 2021

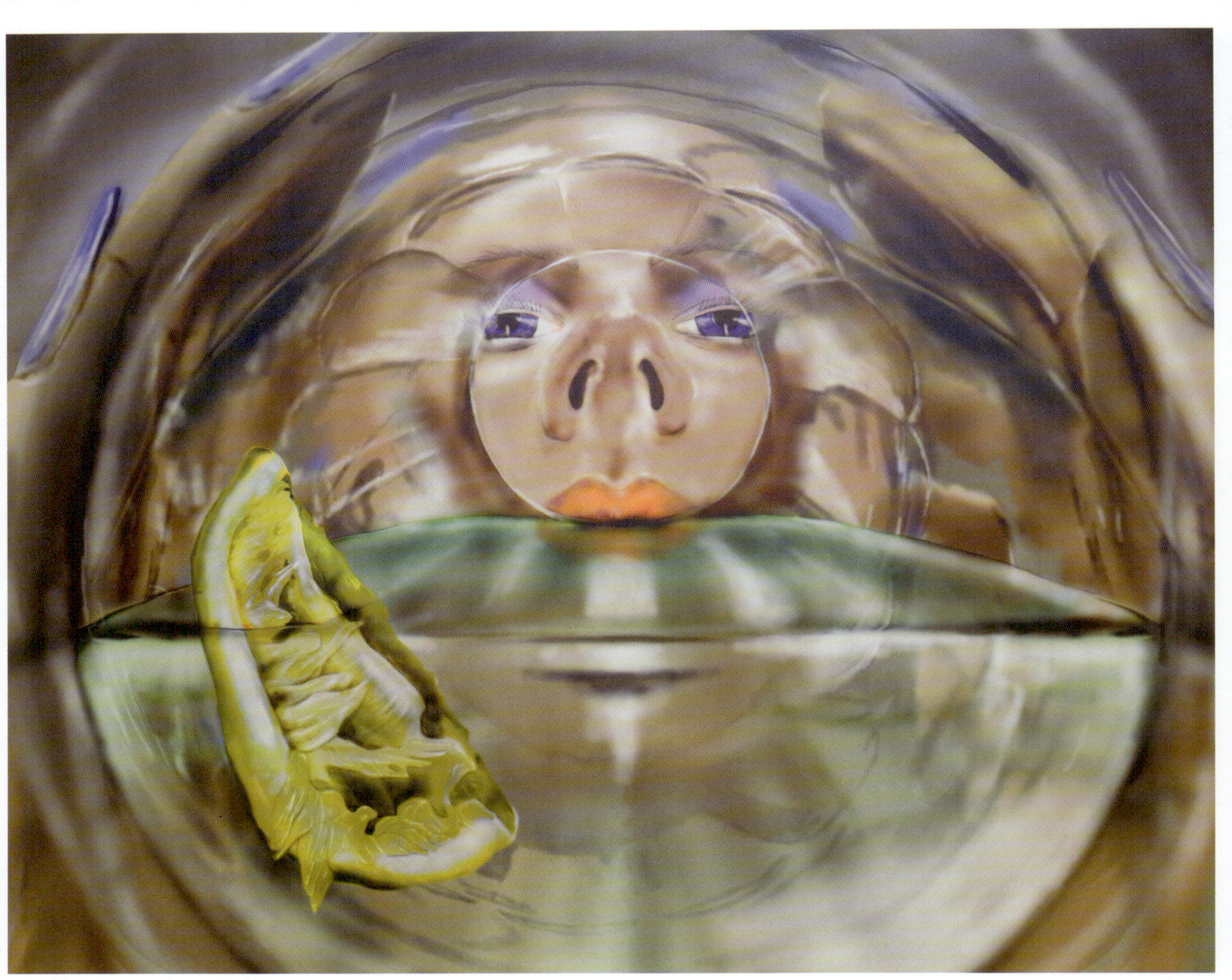

    Thirsty, 2021

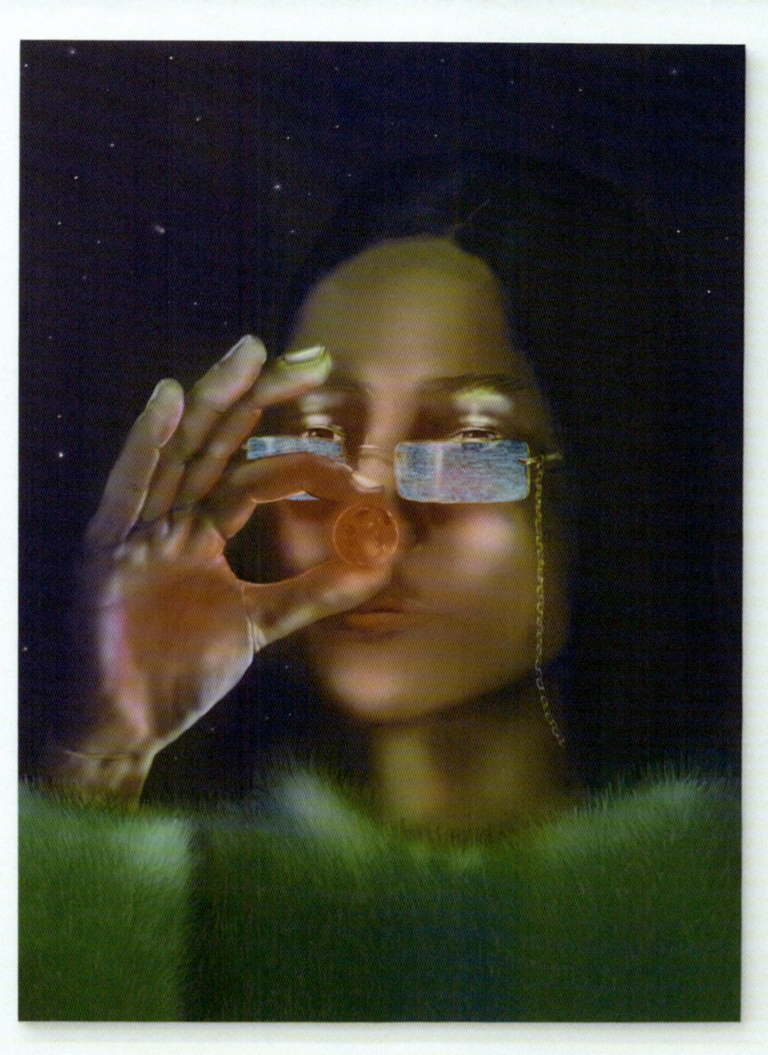

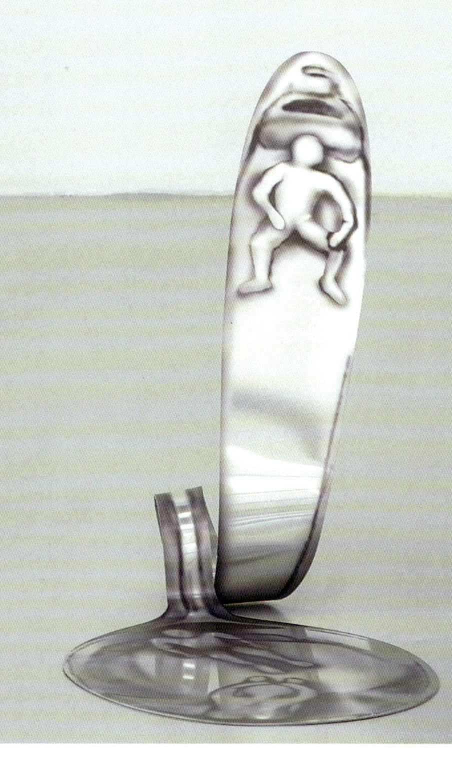

          Spoon 4, 2020   *Blood Moon, 2020*

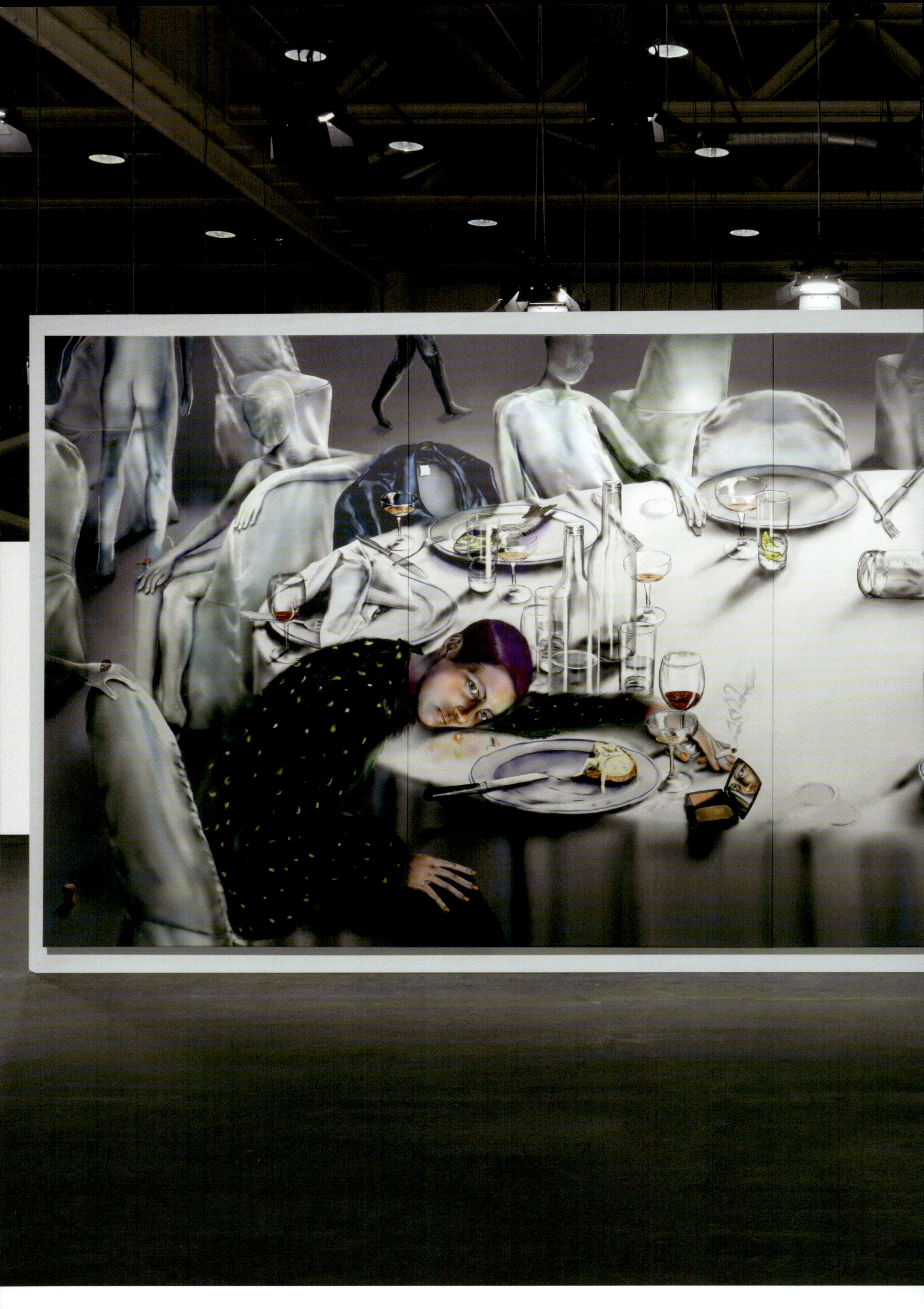

Tête-à-Tête, 2022

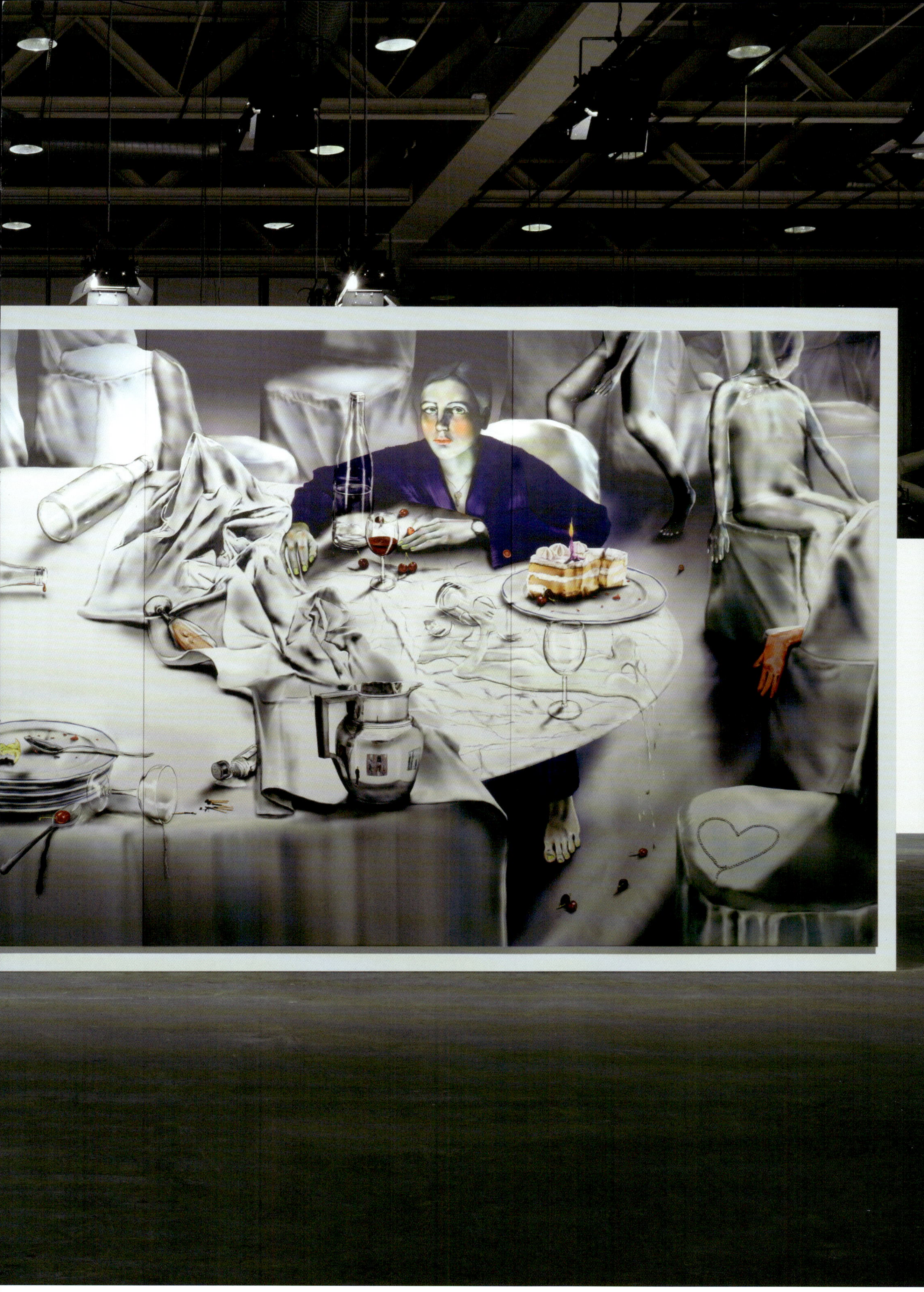

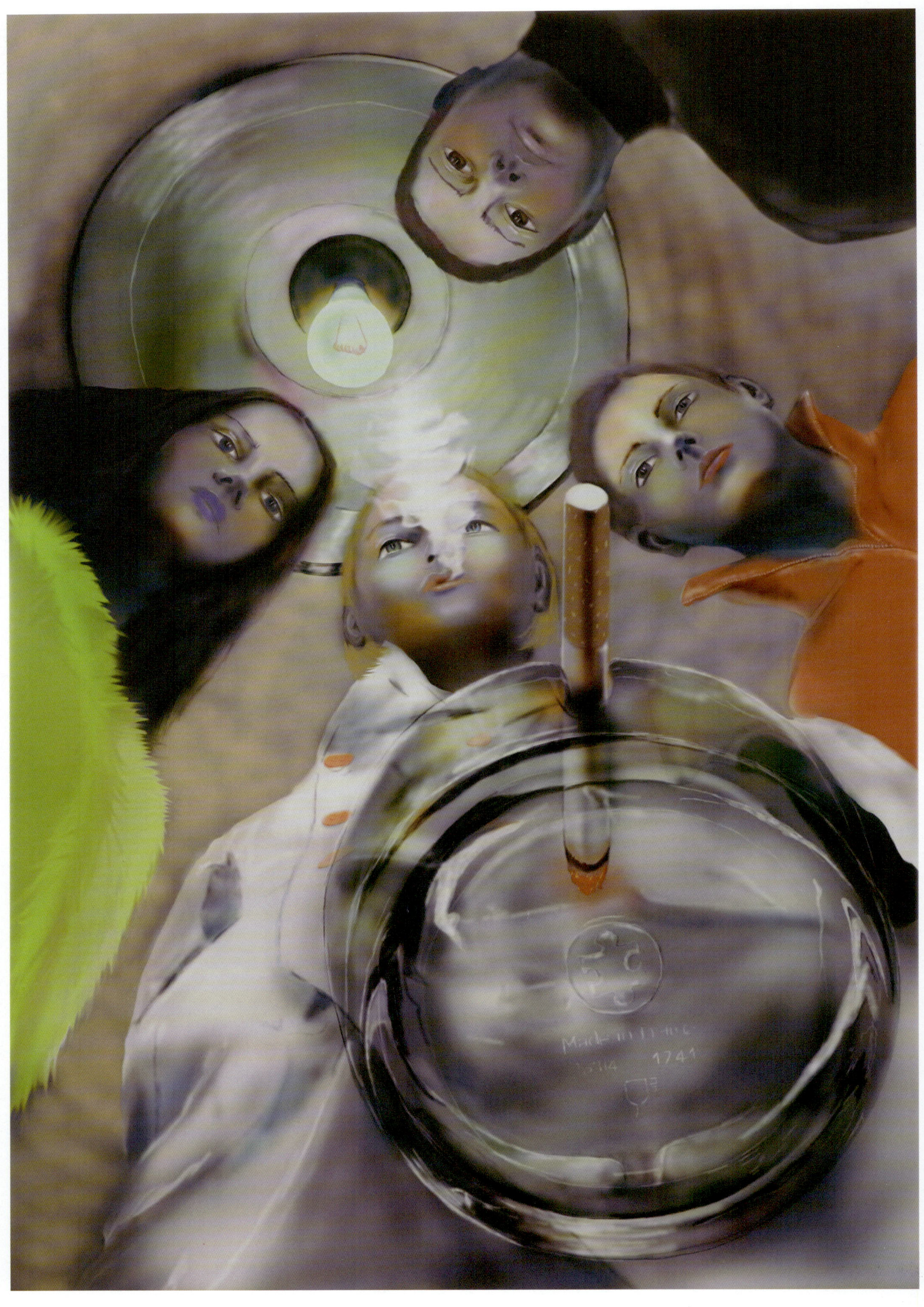

     Under the Table, 2021

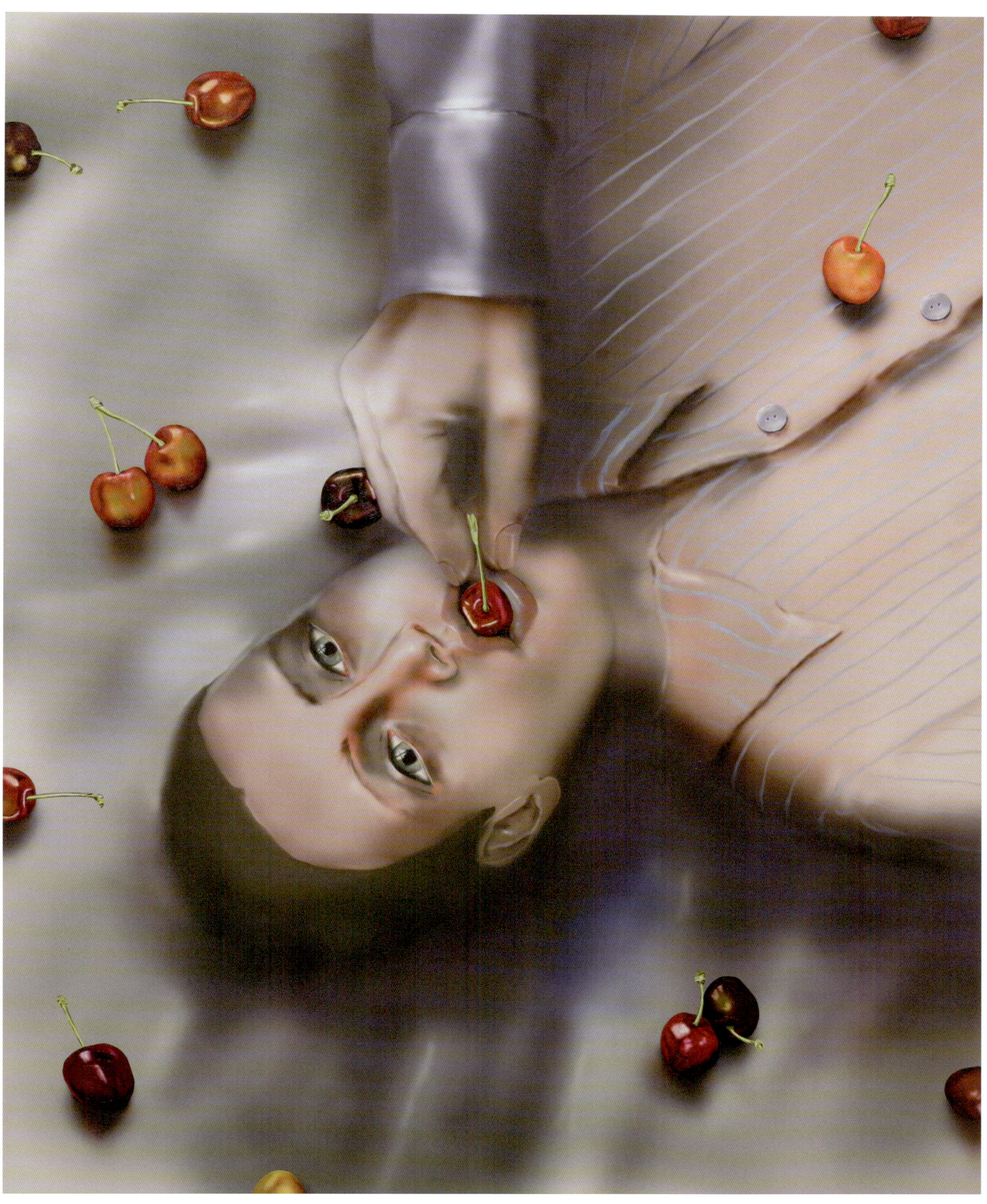

     Treats, 2021

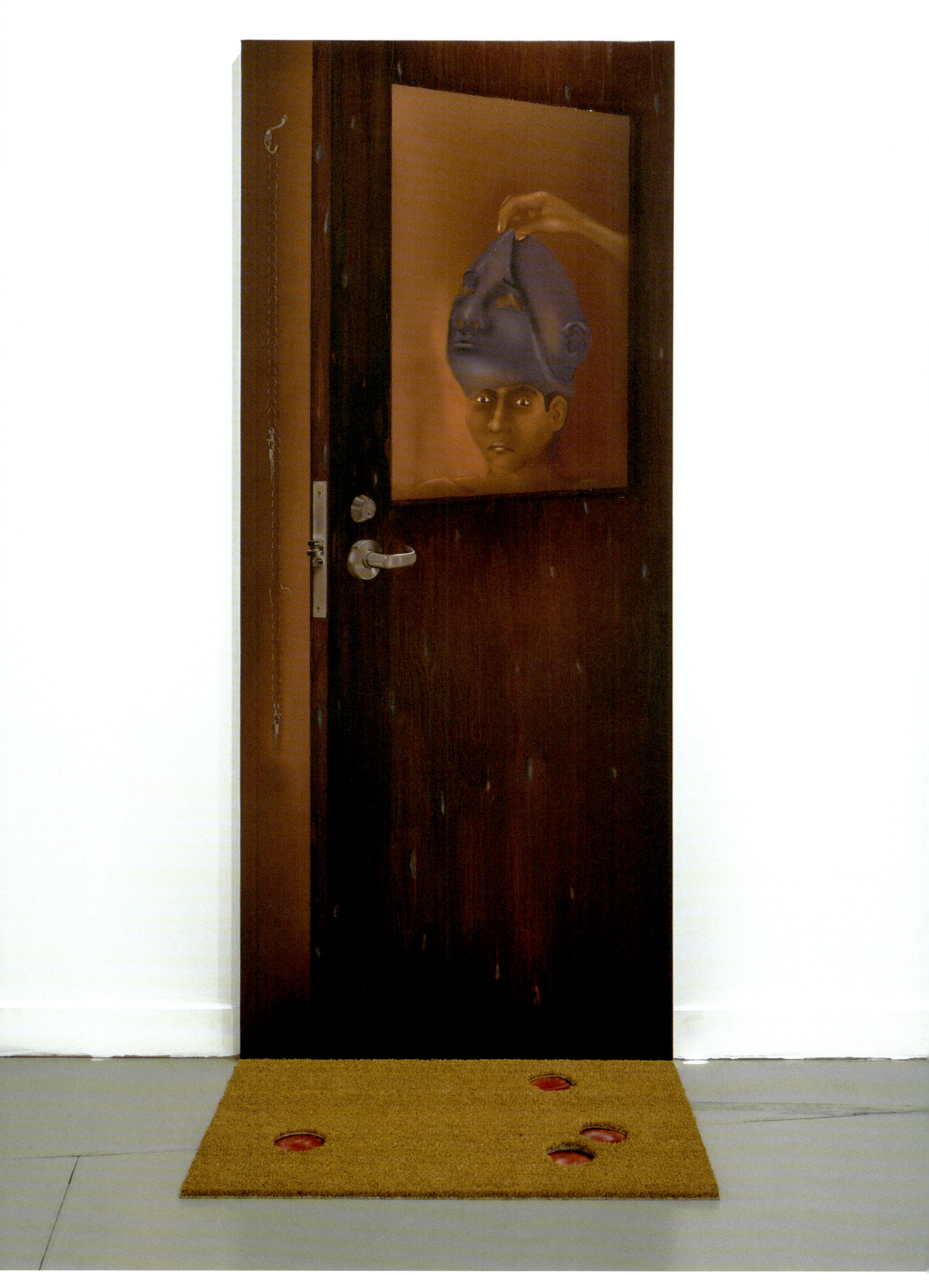

  Face Off, 2019

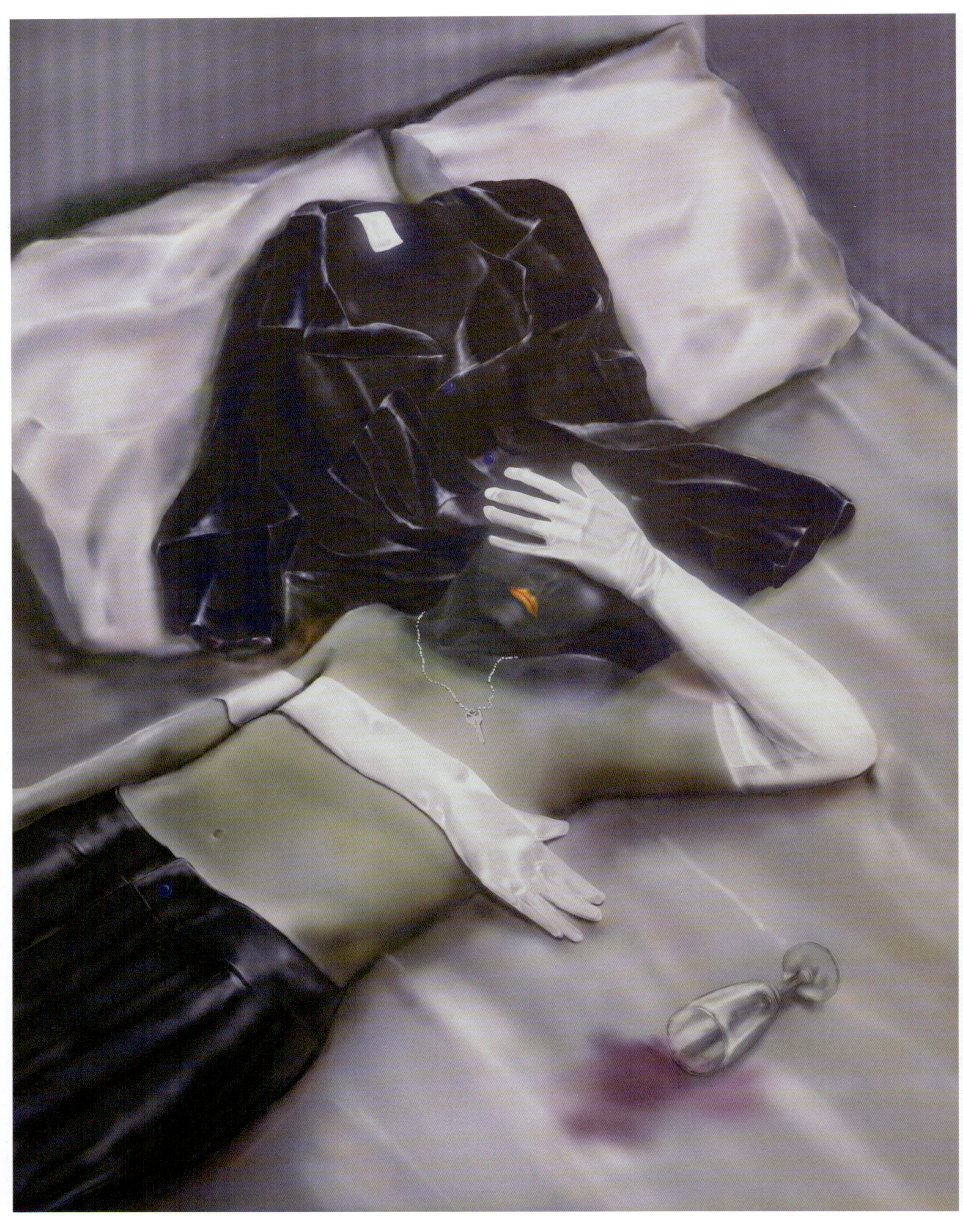

    In the Heat of the Night, 2021

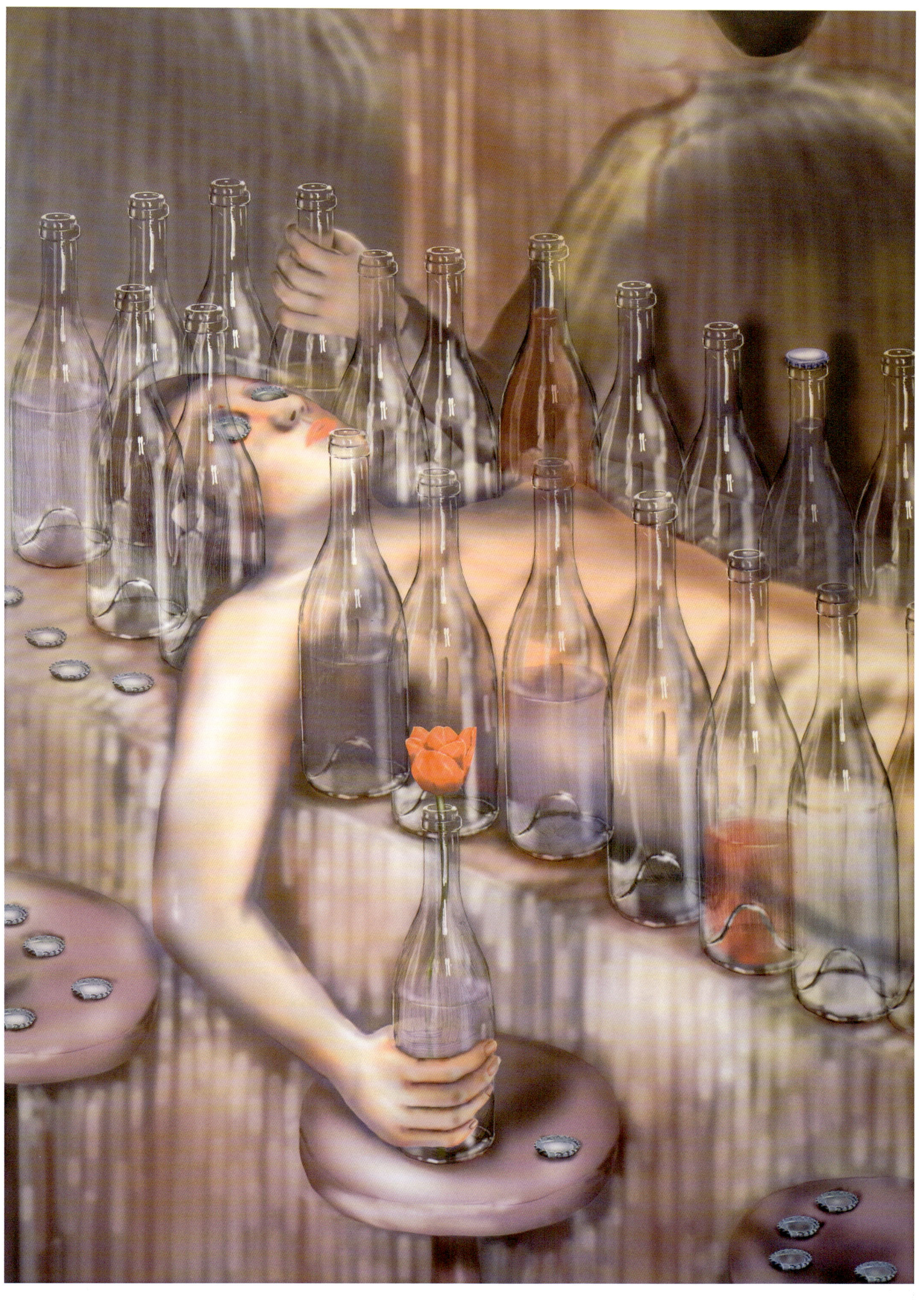

53   *Capped*, 2020

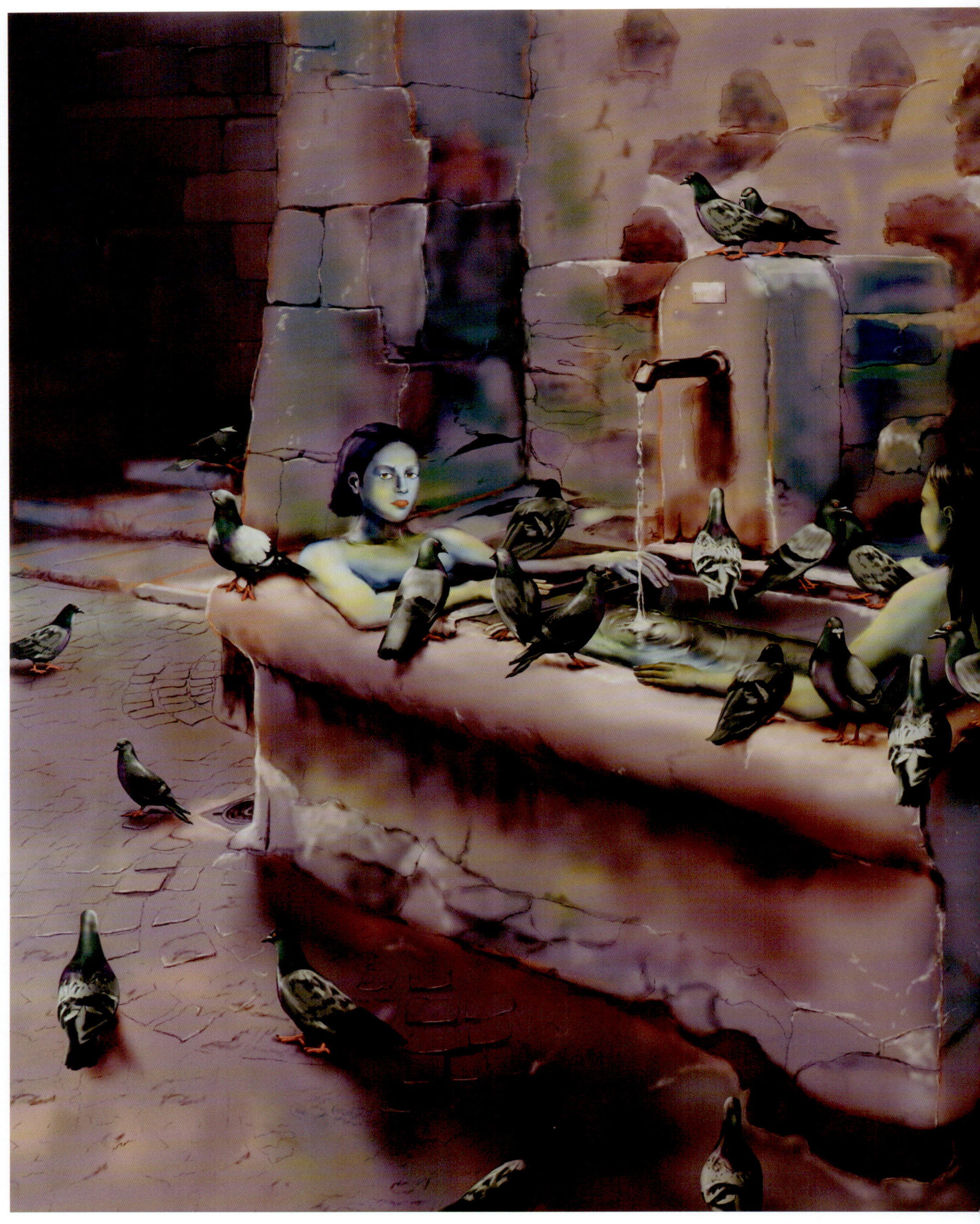

 Open Secret, 2021

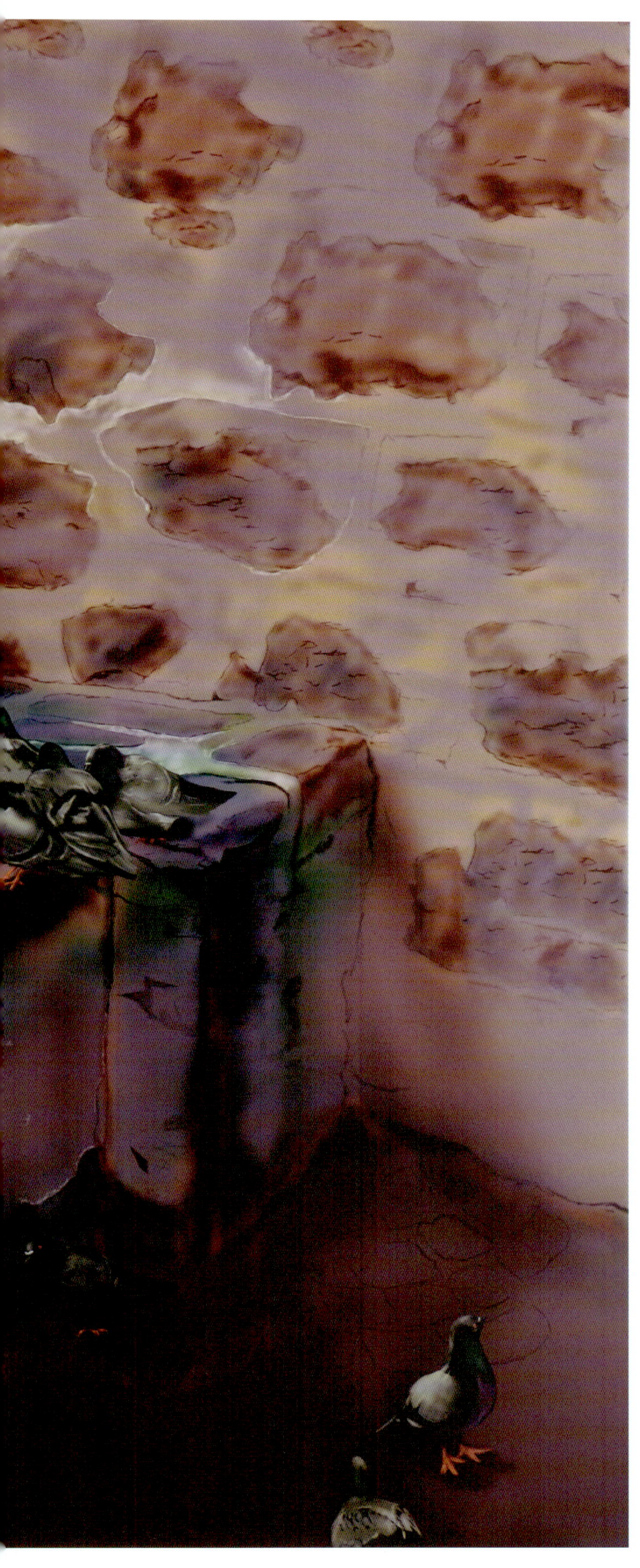

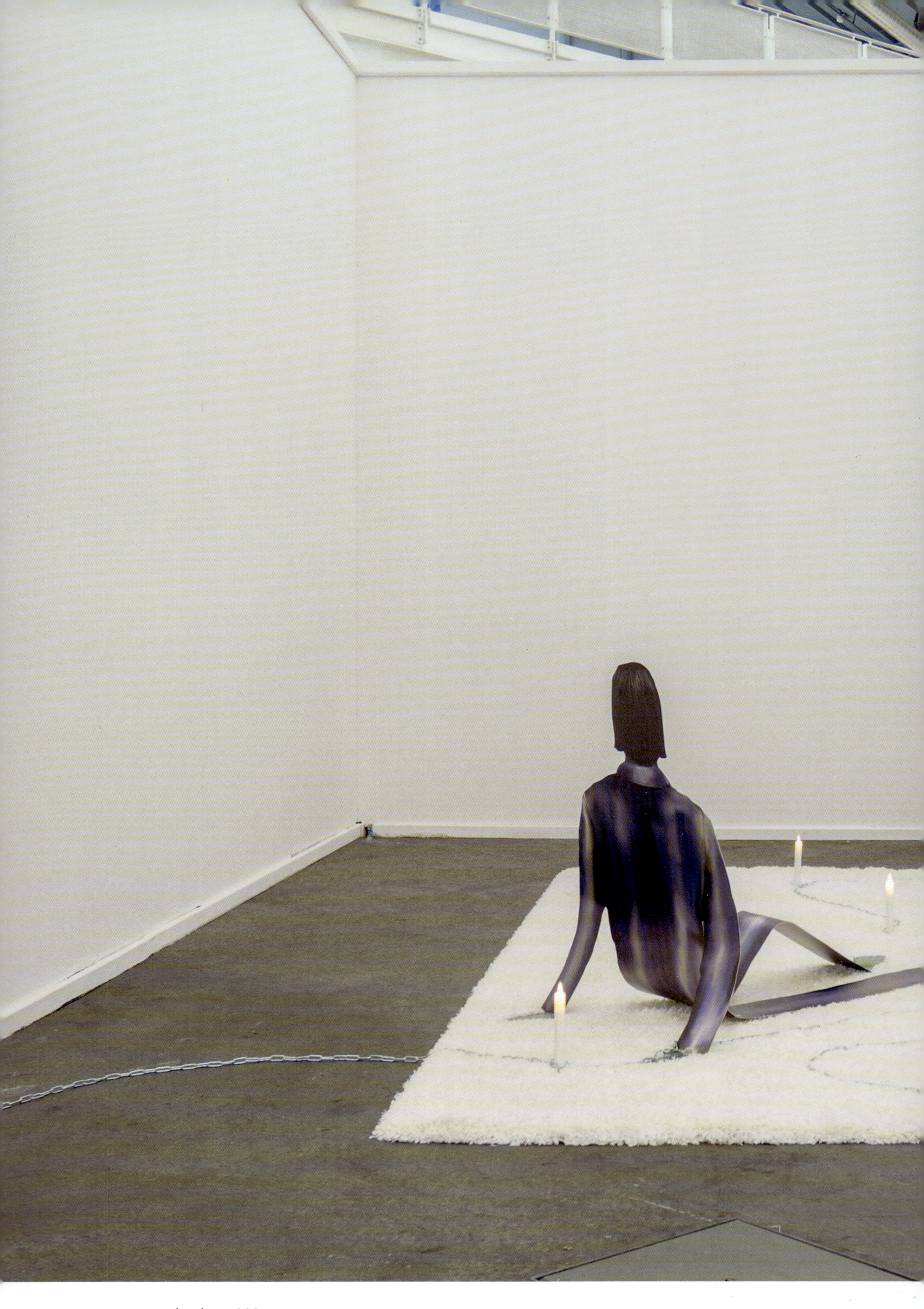

   Permission, 2021

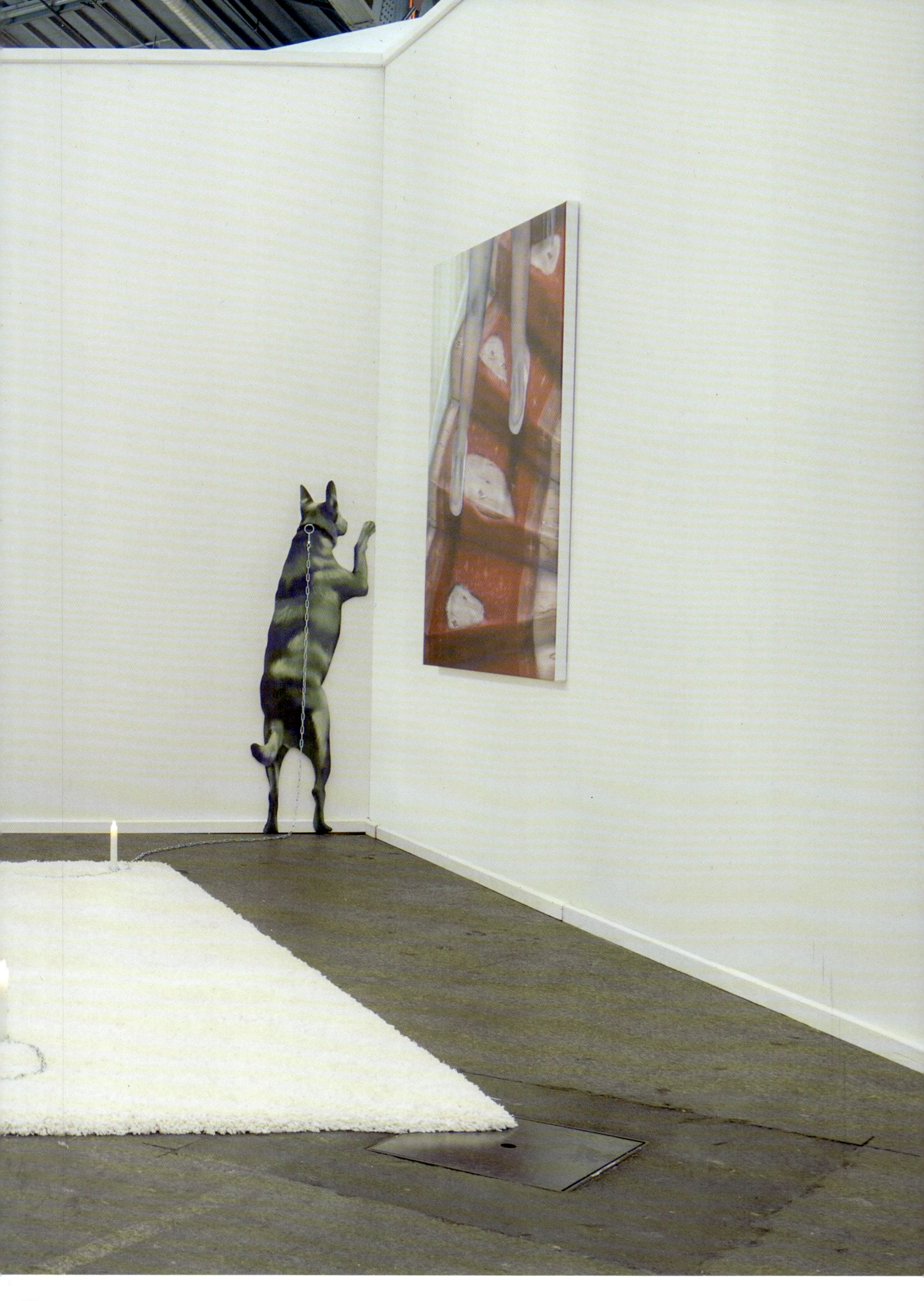

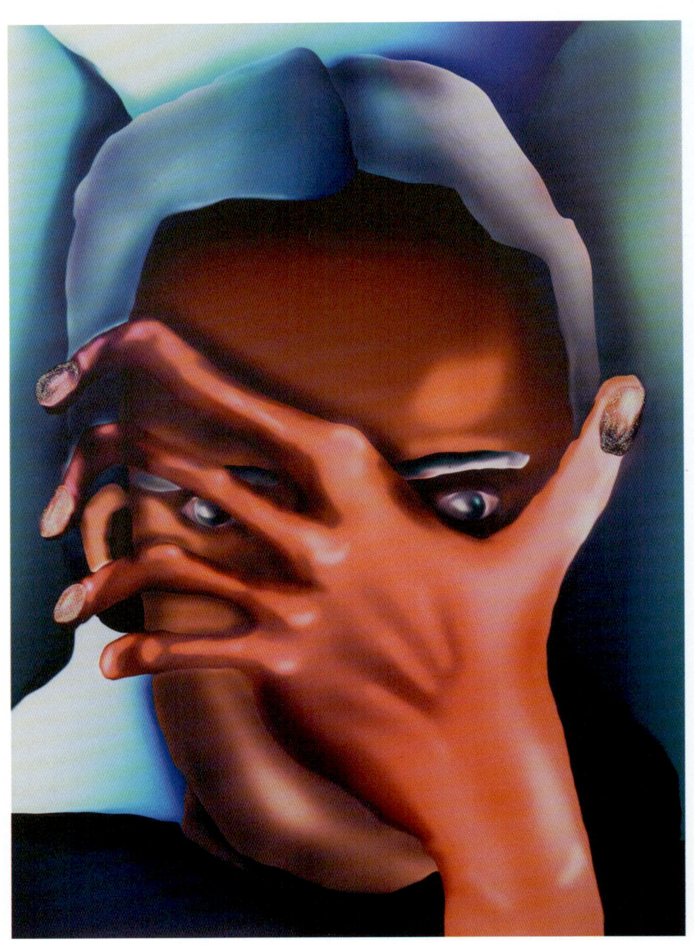

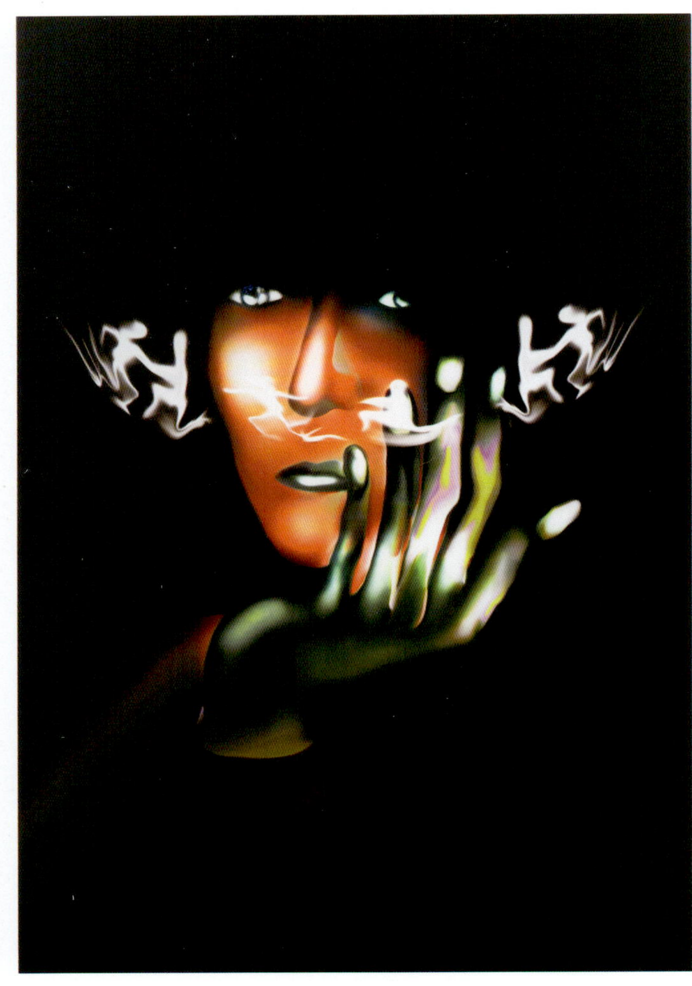

   Still Sleeping, Still Dancing, 2016   *Jo*, 2015

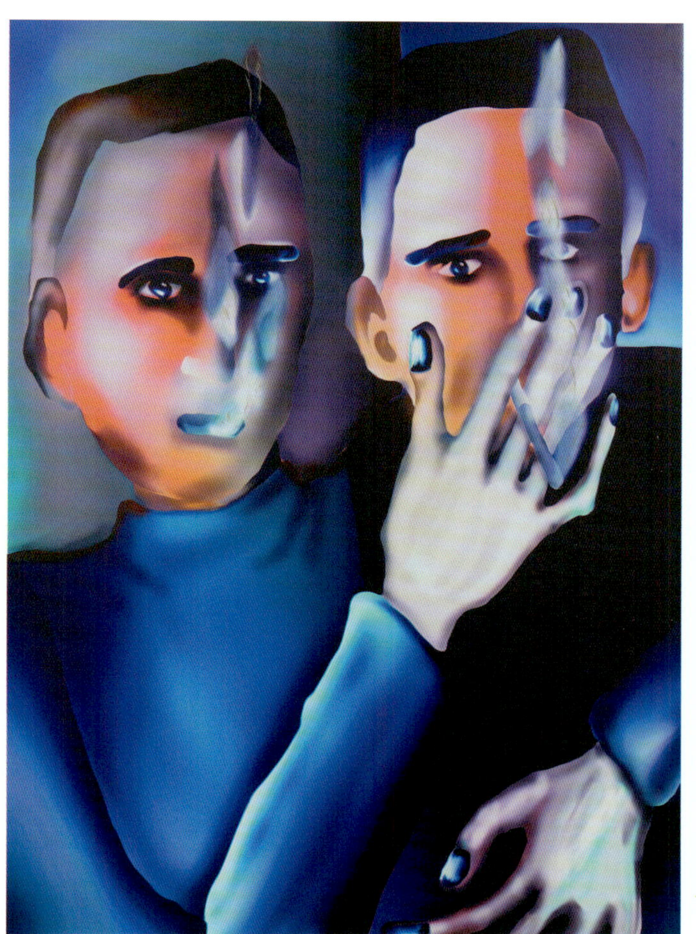
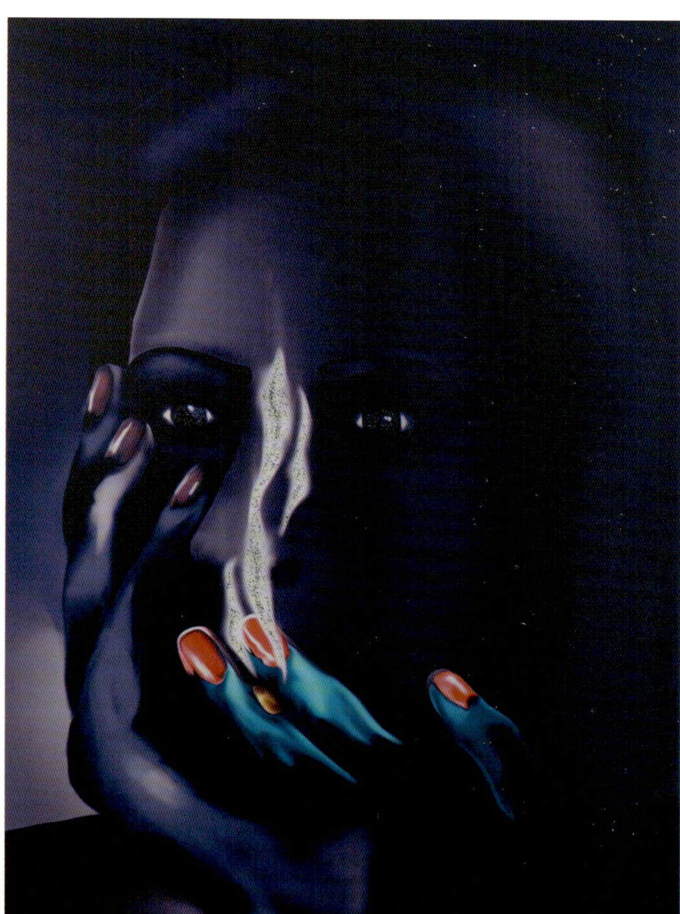
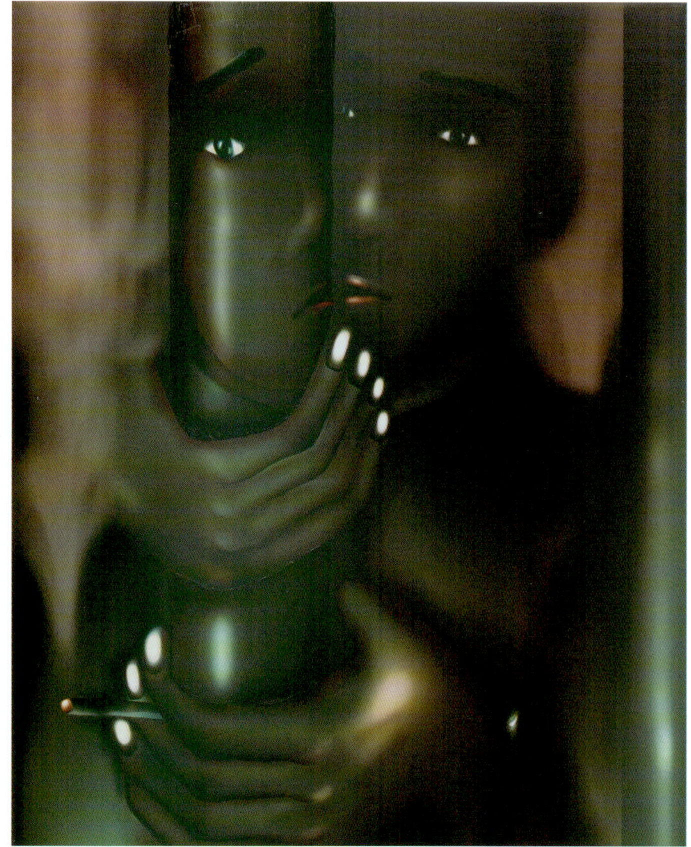

Pierre & Charles, 2015
Untitled, 2016

Charlotte, 2015

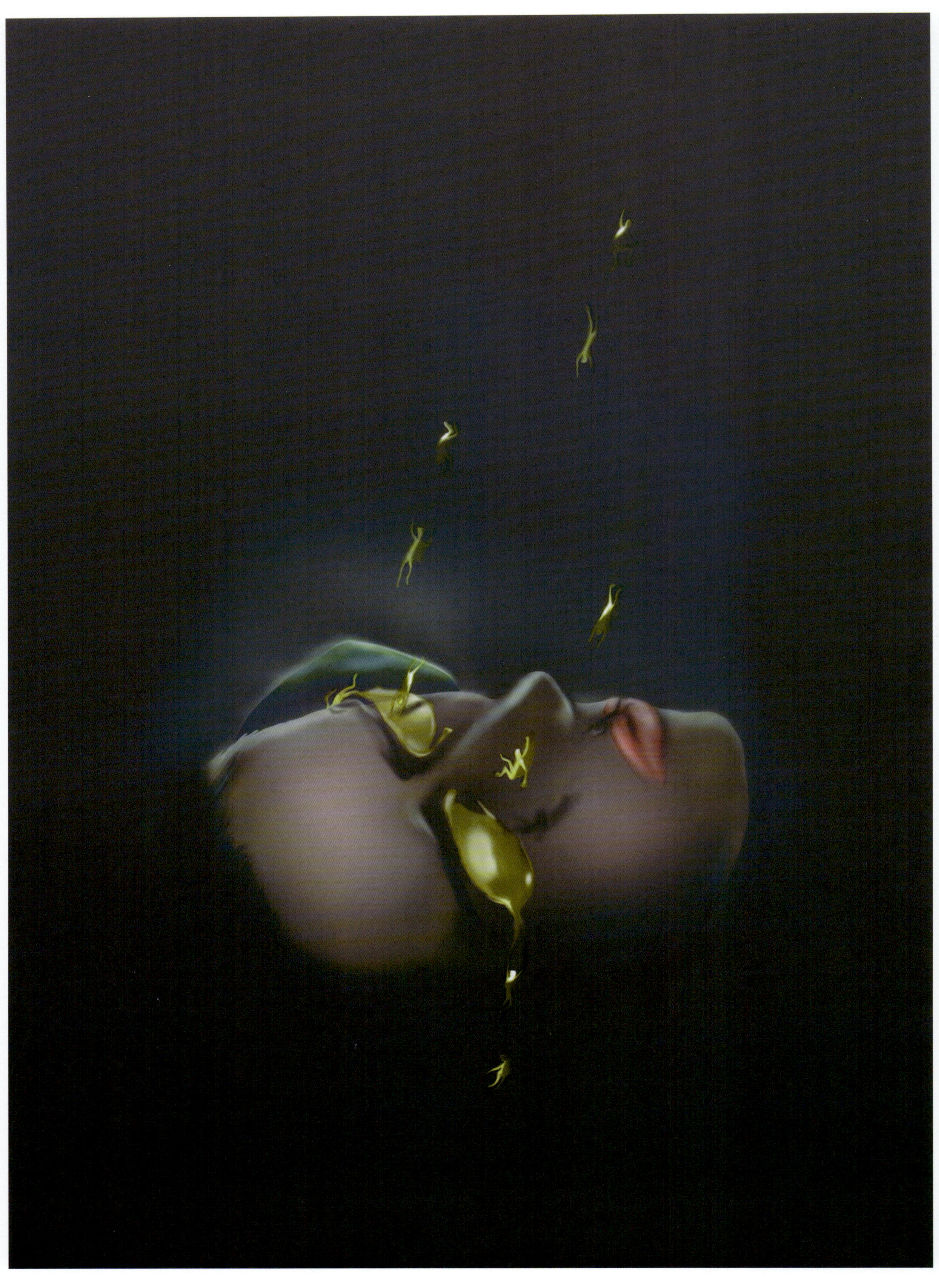

    Under the Weather, 2018

Biography

Born in 1989, Louisa Gagliardi lives in Zurich, Switzerland. She graduated with a BA in Graphic Design from ECAL, Lausanne, in 2012.

She is represented by Rodolphe Janssen, Brussels; Galerie Eva Presenhuber, Zurich, New York, Vienna; and Dawid Radziszewski, Warsaw.

Selected Solo and Two-person Exhibitions

2023
Eva Presenhuber, New York
Galerie Eva Presenhuber, Zurich

2022
Reasonable Doubt, Dawid Radziszewski, Warsaw
Around the Clock, Rodolphe Janssen, Brussels
With Adam Cruces, LEMME, Sion
Louisa Gagliardi, Yves Scherer, Eva Presenhuber, New York

2020
Wishful Thinking, Antenna Space, Shanghai
Raincheck, Dawid Radziszewski, Warsaw

2019
Fruits of Nature, with Adam Cruces, Berlínskej Model, Prague
Side Effects of Satisfaction, Rodolphe Janssen, Brussels
Under the Weather, MOSTYN, Wales

2018
Deleted Scene(s), with Adam Cruces, Joseph Tang, Paris
Holdings, Openforum, Berlin
On a Day Like This, Plymouth Rock, Zurich

2017
Whispers in the Shade, Pilar Corrias, London
Notes for Later, Rodolphe Janssen, Brussels

2016
Walking Errands, with Adam Cruces, The Cabin, Los Angeles

Selected Group Exhibitions

2022
(Un)certain Ground: Current Painting in Switzerland, Kunsthaus Pasqu'art, Biel/Bienne*

2021
Digital Intimacy, National Gallery, Prague
Lemaniana, Centre d'Art contemporain, Geneva
Lugari, Rudimento, Quito

2019
La Métamorphose de l'art imprimé, Verein für Original Graphik, Zurich*
Observer of the Techniques, Wallriss, Fribourg
Dog Days, CLEARING, Brooklyn

2018
On The Road, Aargauer Kunsthaus, Aarau
Tronc Mental, Centre d'art contemporain, Neuchâtel
No Fear of Fainting in a Gym, Kunsthalle, St. Gallen

2017
Being There, Louisiana Museum of Modern Art, Humlebæk*
Mount Analogue, Platform, Stockholm
Werkschau 2017, Museum Haus Kontruktiv, Zurich

2016
Hinter jedem Berg, Helmhaus, Zurich
La Vitesse des images, Instituto Svizzero, Roma

2015
Filter Bubble, Luma Foundation, Zurich
A Form is A Social Gatherer, Plymouth Rock, Zurich

*Publication

Imprint

Editors
Clément Dirié, Arnaud Hubert

Authors
Mitchell Anderson, Simon Castets

Translation from the French
Susan Pickford (Introduction)

Editing and Proofreading
Clare Manchester

Graphic Design
Nicolas Leuba, Nicolas Bolay

Photo Credits
Stefan Altenburger Photography, Zurich;
HV photography; Anders Sune Berg; 幀

Courtesy
Courtesy of the Artist: p. 3, 58t, 59
Courtesy of the Artist and Antenna Space:
p. 2, 4, 26–27, 40, 45
Courtesy of the Artist and Galerie Eva Presenhuber:
p. 5, 6, 8, 12, 41, 48, 54–55
Courtesy of the Artist and Rodolphe Janssen:
p. 14, 15, 16, 17, 19, 24, 25, 29, 30, 58b, 60, 64
Courtesy of the Artist and Dawid Radziszewski:
p. 1, 11, 13, 20–21, 22–23, 28, 32, 39, 42, 43, 44,
49, 51, 52, 53, 56–57
Courtesy of the Artist and Rodolphe Janssen,
Dawid Radziszewski, Galerie Eva Presenhuber:
p. 46–47

Typeface
Unica 77 LL, Unica 77 Mono LL

Cover
Bubble Bath, 2020, detail
Ink on PVC, 130 × 220 cm

Color Separation & Print
Musumeci S.p.A., Quart (Aosta)

Acknowledgments
The artist would like to thank Adam Cruces;
Eva Presenhuber, Christian Schmidt, Andreas Grimm;
Rodolphe Janssen, Julie Senden; Dawid Radziszewski;
Giovanni Carmine; Simon Wang; and Patrice,
Bernadette, Charlotte, Tobias, and Manon Gagliardi.

Printed in Europe.

Published by

JRP|Editions
Rue des Bains 39
CH–1205 Geneva
www.jrp-editions.com

ISBN: 978-3-03764-587-1

JRP|Editions publications are available
internationally at selected bookstores and
from the following distribution partners:

Switzerland
AVA Verlagsauslieferung AG
avainfo@ava.ch
www.ava.ch

Germany and Austria
By JRP|Editions
info@jrp-editions.com
www.jrp-editions.com

France
Les presses du réel
info@lespressesdureel.com
www.lespressesdureel.com

UK and other European countries
Cornerhouse Publications, HOME
publications@cornerhouse.org
www.cornerhousepublications.org

USA, Canada, Asia and Australia
ARTBOOK|D.A.P.
orders@dapinc.com
www.artbook.com

For a list of our partner bookshops or for any
general questions, please contact JRP|Editions
directly at info@jrp-editions.com, or visit our
homepage www.jrp-editions.com for further
information about our program.

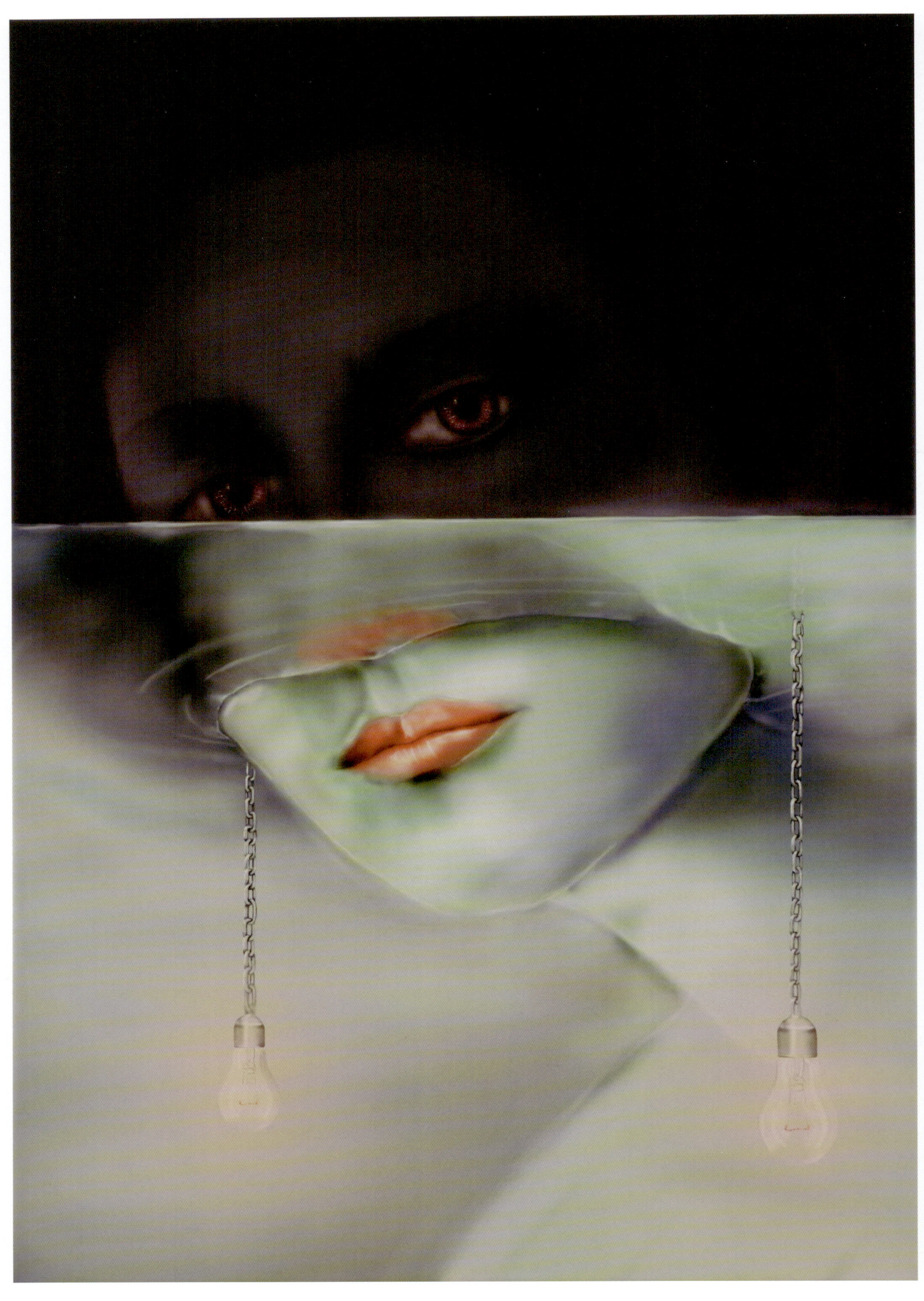

    Taking a Dip, 2021